PRAISE FOR

SONGS OF MY SOUL

God is real! If you don't believe it then read *Songs of My Soul: A Personal Journey to God.* Without a doubt you will see the hand of God at work and how he cares for each of us. In Terry's bold and transparent writing of her own personal trials, tragedies and triumphs you too will find yourself singing your own soul songs on your journey with God.

—Phillip Britt, High School Ministries Pastor, Family Ministries Director at Cary Church of God

SONGS
OF MY SOUL

Caitlin —

Thank you so much
for your skill & expertise
that helped me in my road
to recovery. What a difference
you've made — you were a
God-send. I pray God's
blessings on you & your
career — His favor!
Sincerely —
Jerry

SONGS
OF MY SOUL

A PERSONAL JOURNEY TO GOD

TERRY L. SELLERS

TATE PUBLISHING & *Enterprises*

Published by Tate Publishing & Enterprises, LLC
127 E. Trade Center Terrace | Mustang, Oklahoma 73064 USA
1.888.361.9473 | www.tatepublishing.com

Tate Publishing is committed to excellence in the publishing industry. The company reflects the philosophy established by the founders, based on Psalm 68:11,
"The Lord gave the word and great was the company of those who published it."

Book design copyright © 2010 by Tate Publishing, LLC. All rights reserved.
Cover design by Kellie Southerland
Interior design by Blake Brasor

Published in the United States of America

ISBN: 978-1-61566-589-1
1. Religion, Christian Life, Spiritual Growth
2. Religion, Christian Life, Inspirational
09.12.28

DEDICATION

To the memory of my parents, in honor of their struggles and failures as well as their perseverance and final triumph. Love overlooks any wrong and finds forgiveness. I'm thankful that we shared that kind of love.

ACKNOWLEDGEMENTS

To acknowledge anyone without first giving thanks to my God would just be wrong. There have yet to be written words worthy enough to describe God's goodness to me. Suffice it to say that God is *my everything,* and all else pales in comparison to his great demonstration of mercy and love in my life. It is because of him that I can sing!

From the beginning right until the end of this new endeavor, I have been blessed to have the prayer support of three dear friends: Monica Nichols, Shelby Lowe, and Tara Pish. Ecclesiastes 4:12 says that a cord of three strands is not quickly broken. Together, you have been my cord and I want to thank each of you for your prayers and encouragement along this journey. God expressed his favor on me when he brought you into my life and allowed me to call you my friends.

No such endeavor is done alone and this book would not be complete without the technical help and contributions of some very important people. I need to thank and acknowledge Carolyn Adams, Donna Pitts, Phillip Britt, Shelley Atwell Vasko and Teresa Ball. I value the part each of you made and I appreciate your willingness to help. Thank you seems insufficient but please know that I am truly grateful to each one of you. God's blessings and favor abound in my life.

And how could I overlook Tate Publishing Enterprises for taking a chance on me? Thank you Briana Johnson, Kellie Southerland, Melissa Huffer and everyone I've met along the way, for seeing value in what I have to say and for helping me assemble it into a finished work. You have all been great to work with, patient, and so helpful.

Finally, but certainly not least, I want to thank *all* of my family. Again, words can't express what's in my heart. No matter what life has brought our way, it has always brought us back together. Thank each one of you for your contribution and investment in my life. Friends are different because they choose to be friends or not. With family, it's not a choice; it just is. If I had to choose who my family would be, there's not a single one of you I would leave out, including you, Selena, Ashley, Sean, and John. I love you all so, so much!

TABLE
OF CONTENTS

FOREWORD

The complexities of today's modern life lead many people toward a path of darkness. The slumping economy, rising gas prices, housing market woes, high divorce rates, and other issues in our society leave us all vulnerable to the dark path. Many are not able to get past these obstacles in life. People need constant affirmation and motivation just to do the right thing. In my opinion, a true story, an inspiration, if you will, filled with hope helps people overcome extraordinary circumstances, all those things associated with our modern lifestyle.

Terry Sellers has experienced despair, pain, and even humiliation at the hands of those she trusted most in her life. While reading this, I found myself screaming for someone to help her. Couldn't anyone see what she was going through, or was there just a day in and day out monotony? Life goes on. We are alive; we go to church three times each week—nothing needs to change. Hopelessness abounded for Terry, yet she endured. What gave her that hope to go forward when so many things were so wrong in her young life? In writing her book, she has a sense of purpose. She wants people to see the despair her heart has endured and the final triumph from destruction and into a path with God.

Songs of My Soul: A Personal Journey to God is a poignant journey through hurt and heartache. It has not been an easy journey for her. While some may question why she wrote this personal account and relived very painful moments in her life, you must know that it was something Terry felt God asked of her.

When we follow God's words, he heals the hurt and fixes what is broken. No one knows your frustration, hurt, or anger better than him. Terry's personal story is a testament to that. Life is not perfect, nor is it painless, but you have to trust in God to lead you along that path. God has a plan and a purpose for each of us. Perhaps by sharing what she has overcome, Terry will serve as an inspiration for you to choose the right path, as that is her intention and hope. It's not her path but the one God intends for each of you!

> Trust in the *Lord* with all your heart and lean not on your own understanding; in all your ways acknowledge him, and he will make your paths straight.
>
> Proverbs 3:5–6

—Donna L. Pitts, Au.D
Assistant Clinical Professor, Loyola University, MD

INTRODUCTION

So, what's up with this title? you may wonder. Please allow me to explain. Since I've never written a book, I wondered just where to start and realized that the title is probably as good of a place as any. Speaking of the title, don't let me mislead you. I'm not a musician. Nope. I'm not even a songwriter or a singer. While none have ever offered me money *to sing*, some have offered me money *not* to sing, but I have a song in my heart, and I just can't keep from singing.

So why the title? It's simple really. From as early as I can remember, I have believed in God. It's as if I could always feel his presence near me. This book is really more about the subtitle than the title, my personal journey to God and how that journey made my soul sing. More specifically, the first half of my life has been a journey *to* God and the second half of my life has been a journey *with* God. Believe me my life hasn't been one without lots of mistakes and hardships. I'm no different than you are in that respect. In fact, my life compared to yours may seem like the Zip-A-Dee-Doo-Dah song.

I'm not writing this because I desire to compare

my life with yours or because I desire to make myself vulnerable as I share the details of my life with you. And this book certainly won't hold life's answers, only the wisdom I gained along the way. Ronald Reagan said it best when he stated, "Within the covers of the Bible are the answers for all the problems men face." You'll find my number one source in the pages that follow is, in fact, the Bible. My purpose in this lies in the desire to tell you about my God and what he's done in my life in hopes that it will somehow encourage you. To me, there really is no true life apart from God. Had it not been for God, I wouldn't be here to write my story today.

Having said all of that let me also say that I do love music. Who doesn't? It is such a dynamic force with the power to move us. Music makes us *feel*, and it allows us to express those feelings. I'm willing to bet that you can't recall a major event in your life where music wasn't some aspect of that memory. We can hear a certain song and immediately be transported to some place in our past, whether it's good or bad. Take any movie ever made; remove the musical score, and the script loses so much of its impact. I bet I can make you feel the forlorn and suspense by just saying "Jaws" as a certain scene starts to play in your mind and you hear the music, foretelling doom ahead. And what would the scene from *Gone with the Wind* be like as Scarlett takes in the desolation of her beloved Tara without the music to set the mood?

Music has a way of telling a story. It gets down into our souls. I can't look at creation without thinking about my God or his majestic power, which brings

TERRY L. SELLERS

to mind my favorite song of all: "How Great Thou Art" by Stuart K. Hine. Just this past summer, I experienced such a moment as a group of us were flying home from a mission trip in Ecuador. Due to severe storms in Georgia and the Carolinas, our flight was delayed several hours in Miami. By the time we finally boarded our plane and took off, it was well after midnight, and many people were resting. Not me. I was looking out of the plane's window, enthralled as we flew just above a storm.

The display of God's power was so awesome. The sky would flash as lighting would outline the soft, billowing clouds for several seconds as far as the eye could see. Then all would go black as the night enfolded the scene only to replay it again seconds later. I was privy to this spectacular display for about ten minutes as the words to that song rang in my mind:

> Oh Lord my God! when I in awesome wonder
> Consider all the worlds Thy hands have made;
> I see the stars, I hear the rolling thunder,
> Thy pow'r throughout the universe displayed!:
> Then sings my soul, my Savior God to Thee
> HOW GREAT THOU ART!

Well, that's what I want to do. I want to tell you my story through the use of songs. In each chapter of my life, there was a specific song that I could identify with, a song that revealed a part of my soul. I use the lyrics to set the stage and to express that particular chapter of my life. Music dates back to the beginning of time. The Bible is full of references to music and songs of praise. In fact, the longest book of the Bible

is Psalms. In Hebrew, *psalms* means *praises*; in Greek, the word means *songs to the accompaniment of stringed instruments*. When you read the Bible, you'll discover that there are many songs written in the pages thereof, but you'll also find that they weren't always a song of praise. Sometimes it was a song of deep despair or a song sung out of fear.

The singers weren't always particularly happy to be in the places they were in. For example, I'm sure you're familiar with the story of King Jehoshaphat in 2 Chronicles 20 when Jehoshaphat's front line of defense in a battle against Ammon, Moab, and Mount Seir was men singing and praising God. Just imagine that. Now, I don't know about you, but if I were going into battle—and especially if I were going to be on the *front lines*—I would much rather have a weapon in my hand than a trumpet. But that's just me. Call me crazy.

My point here is that my soul's song has not always been an uplifting one, nor has it always been from the best of circumstances. That's not to say that my life has been all bad. No. I have been truly blessed, even through the bad times, and I am thankful to my God. I will tell you that part of my story is due to things that happened to me—more specifically, things that happened in my home and by my parents.

Can I just inject a side note here? It is not my intention to point out the bad in anyone through my story, and especially not in my parents. They were not bad people. They provided for me and raised me the best they knew how. But no one is born into greatness. No one starts out life with all of the answers; we

TERRY L. SELLERS

figure it out as we go, and we learn mostly from our mistakes. Often, we hurt those we love along the way. Sometimes life throws so many obstacles so fast that it merely becomes about just surviving, let alone caring for and loving those around you, even your own children.

There were bad things that happened to me, hurtful things, and my parents were sometimes the cause of that. I am not saying anything accusingly, condemningly, or judgmentally. I am simply trying to tell things as they happened. This is really more a story about God's mercy and grace in my life and in the lives of my parents, but I first have to share the uncomfortable places. It is not out of anger that I write these things. I loved my parents, and they loved me—all through our brokenness.

I'm not pretending to be this girl who has had a lifetime of woes caused by others. No. I realize that we're all sinners. Ecclesiastes 7:20 says, "There is not a righteous man on earth who does what is right and never sins." My story may speak some awful truths, but please stick around to read the end of the story. This is really about my God, *my everything*, and what he can do in a life that accepts his forgiveness and mercy.

In this book, I want to open a window to my soul, if you will, to be very transparent with you as I share some painful moments. Why? Well, maybe you've walked where I have, yet you still struggle. Maybe something I have to say can help you. Maybe your soul's song is still a sad one. I recently heard it said that a wise man learns from his mistakes but an even wiser man learns from the mistakes of others. I've made lots

of mistakes along the way, and I'm sure there are more to come, but I pray that somehow my life can help touch another life—perhaps your life—for the good, for eternity. Maybe, just maybe, I can save you some footsteps of pain as I share where I've already walked.

In my life, there are two things I've come to know for sure. First, there is a God who loves me. I call him "my everything" because he is. I can't think of a better name, nor can I imagine life apart from God. Second, there is an enemy who is determined to take my soul's song and even my very soul. You can call him Satan, Lucifer, the devil, or whatever. I call him "liar" because that's how he works best in all of our lives. The Bible actually calls him the father of all lies. In fact, he first made his debut on earth—as a snake, deceiving Eve in the garden.

Did you know that, in heaven, Satan was actually the most beautiful angel and in charge of the music? I find that interesting because now he works hard to take away the songs of the saints, to keep them so suppressed they often lose their praise. Why? Because he knows that there is power in music and especially power in praise to the one true God. The name *Satan* itself means *to obstruct*. In reality, that's all he can do—whisper lies to us and hope we believe them so he obstructs our reality of God. I know I believed him. Let me share.

TERRY L. SELLERS

NURSERY RHYME DAYS

Music is what feelings sound like.

—Unknown

I was born and raised in a small town in southeastern North Carolina named Whiteville. My family consisted of my parents, an older brother, myself, and a younger sister and brother. In the earlier days of my life, most of my memories were good. There were holidays celebrated with family and friends, playing games together, family vacations, and even meals together—a novelty now. It was a place and time where you felt safe enough to leave your doors unlocked and unannounced visits from the neighbors were welcomed. Maybe it was because I lived in the South, or maybe it was just the way things used to be.

As a child, I loved to sing. My mom once told me that I was always singing something from the time I could talk. Maybe I took after her in that respect because one thing I remember from my childhood and youth is hearing my mom sing or hum as she worked around the house or carried on daily life. Christmas

was usually a joyful time in our home and all the more reason to sing. One of the most memorable Christmas gifts I recall was this little, portable record player with a nicely boxed set of nursery rhyme songs on forty-fives. My favorite song was "I'm a Little Teapot."

Now, to those of you who actually know me and the song, you know that I'm neither short nor stout, and I'm certainly not a teapot. But I have been known to get steamed up and shout. So, why was this my soul's song? This song represents the earliest memories of my life. I was a child, and I had no worries, just happy and carefree.

In our backyard, there was this tree house that my dad built for us. My parents would often have fish fries on the weekends and invite family and friends over. I recall nights in that tree house with my little record player and stack of forty-fives, just singing away. It was a time of innocence in my life.

There's so much I remember with fondness, but one thing I don't recall was much demonstration of love or display of emotions in my home. Don't get me wrong, we were close in our own way. My dad's family mostly lived in Fayetteville in the early years of my life, and we would visit them often on the weekends. They were good people, but looking back, I can see that there were a lot of problems in his family, a lot of broken lives. Addiction to alcohol was the biggest factor. It destroyed several of his siblings' marriages and his own. That didn't change the fact that we were family and we loved each other, or the fact that they were and still are good people. Getting together with my cousins was so much fun.

TERRY L. SELLERS

My mom's family lived in Baltimore, and we usually spent our summer and often our Christmas vacations there. The summers usually meant trips to the Baltimore Zoo or to Hershey Park, a family favorite. My mom's family would also spend their summer vacations with us or nearby at the coast. There would be day trips between Myrtle Beach and White Lake. I can't think of more loving, giving people. They have always been a support for me and my family. Family was important in our home, regardless of any problems. Mostly, life was what you called *good* when I was a child.

I don't know exactly when things began to change, but I'm sure that it had a lot to do with my dad's growing addiction to alcohol. My mom was what people call a Christian; my Dad wasn't. What that meant was that she was human, but she tried her best to live a life pleasing to God, according to the Bible. She also tried to raise her children that way. With time, my dad's drinking became worse; so did life for my family. I recall nights when he would come home late. He and my mom would fight. I would hear him cursing, throwing things, and even beating her. I would lie in bed afraid to even move, afraid that I might be next. Don't get me wrong. My dad wasn't normally a scary man, but alcohol turned him into a monster to be feared.

Many nights, my dad wouldn't come home at all—maybe to avoid the fighting. Sometimes in the wee hours of the night, my mom would awaken us four children and load us into the old blue station wagon to drive from bar to bar looking for him. She was fighting

for her family the best way she knew how. When she found him, the scene was usually ugly.

On Sundays and Wednesdays, my mom would also load us four children into that same car and take us to church. I remember listening to her sing all the way home from services. She seemed truly happy, and I would wonder how she could sing. I lived in the same house. I also recall walking past her bedroom and the door being open just enough for me to see her on her knees in prayer and to hear her calling out to God for her husband and for her children.

Even with that, as far back as my memory goes, I recall being told things such as "You don't think," or, "You can't do anything right." (There he is, the liar!) I don't recall much affirmation or praise from either of my parents—only criticism. I often wondered if my parents loved me. I considered myself the black sheep of the family.

Outside of my home, life could be cruel also. I'm sure you've all heard the cliché, "Sticks and stones may break my bones, but words will never hurt me." How untrue is that? Sometimes words hurt the most. The Bible says in Proverbs 18:21 that the power of life and death are in the tongue. I once heard someone put it this way: "David defeated Goliath with sticks and stones, but mere words have defeated thousands."

It seemed like no matter where I went, people were so quick to point out my faults. I was called names like Freckle Face, Snow Beach, Big Foot—the list goes on. Maybe the name-calling was all in fun, but it had a very negative impact. I began to see only the bad in me, and I developed a poor self-image. I also devel-

TERRY L. SELLERS

oped a lifelong fight with negative thinking. I believed what everyone else was saying but that was the liar again, hard at work. That's why I think it's important to teach children to respect others, especially with their words, even other children. You never know what is going on in a person's life or what an impact your spoken words can have. I would much rather speak something positive to a person than something negative. I will never forget those who spoke kind, uplifting words to me or those who didn't, but I'll get off of my soapbox now and get back to my story.

Altogether, this made me think, *If I am so bad, why does God love me as I have been taught in Sunday school for years?* I felt so unlovable and unloved. I was beginning to walk in defeat, and I was only a child. I truly believed in God and felt a deep love for him, but I was starting down a path on which I would soon get lost.

Like I said before though, life wasn't all bad. I was blessed to have a comfortable living. I had a normal childhood in that I played dolls with my best friend, I rode bikes with my big brother, and I played house with my younger siblings and friends. My parents would go out in the yard and play with us kids. They would play basketball with me. It was my favorite. My dad used to take us skating on the weekends, and my mom would take us and our friends swimming during the hot, summer days. There were even a number of years when Daddy's drinking wasn't so bad. Our family shared lots of laughs and good memories along the way; we had much to be thankful for.

But one night in the late seventies, things changed. My dad was intoxicated, and he was driving my broth-

er's newly purchased, yet used motorcycle. My brother was riding on the back with him when Daddy lost control and wrecked. Thankfully, God spared both of their lives. My brother was okay—just minor injuries—but Daddy broke his back and had to go through multiple surgeries. He became disabled for a while and couldn't work. Eventually, what savings my parents had became depleted, and Daddy couldn't provide for his family anymore. After he and my mom had sold everything they could to pay the bills, including their wedding bands, he had to apply for welfare. I think that was the final blow to his pride. That's when life really began to change, as did my soul's song. Gone were the days of innocence and the little nursery rhyme songs.

TERRY L. SELLERS

LONESOME
LOSER

Have you heard about the Lonesome Loser?
Beaten by the Queen of Hearts every time.
Have you heard about the Lonesome Loser?
He's a loser but he still keeps on trying.
Sit down, take a look at yourself
Don't you want to be somebody?
Someday somebody's gonna see inside
You have to face up, you can't run and hide.
Unlucky at love at least that's what they say
He lost his head and he gambled his heart away
He still keeps searching though there's nothing left
Staked his heart and lost, now he has to pay the cost.
"It's okay." He smiles and says
But this loneliness is driving him crazy.
He don't show what goes on in his head
But if you watch very close you'll see it all.
Sit down, take a look at yourself
Don't you want to be somebody?
Someday somebody's gonna see inside
You have to face up, you can't run and hide.
Have you heard about the Lonesome Loser?
Now tell me have you heard about the Lonesome Loser?

—David Briggs

> Music and rhythm find their way into the secret places of the soul.
>
> —Plato

I don't have to tell you how important the teenage years are in a person's life. It's a time when we're all trying to find an identity for ourselves, to find a place we fit. By the time I had reached my teenage years, my self-identity was one of a loser. Even though I had a lot of friends, I was so lonely inside. I could identify with the song "Lonesome Loser."

On the outside, most people would look at me and just think I was average, that life was okay. In reality, my world was falling apart, but I couldn't tell anyone. I felt trapped and scared. I would lie in bed at night and beg God to take me out of the situation. Life was cruel.

A person's home is supposed to be a safe haven, yet mine had become its own personal hell. I was being sexually abused by my dad, and I was afraid to tell my mom. Although my mom was a Christian, she was human, and she often said things to me that were negative. In ways, she used me as an outlet for her own aggression, and I was really afraid of her. Once, she told me that I was her strongest child and that she knew she didn't have to worry about me. That may have been true, but there's a difference between being strong and just being stoic. Strong I was not, but maybe that is why I was her outlet.

There wasn't a trusting mother-daughter relationship between us, and I never went to her with my problems. So, when the abuse started, in my mind, I

TERRY L. SELLERS

couldn't tell her. It would all be my fault. The fear of what would happen to me if the truth became known was as bad as the abuse itself and kept me in this world of secrets and such pain. I had seen my dad's fury unleashed on my mom, and I had been the recipient of my mom's frustrations as they were sometimes unleashed on me. I wanted to run away, but as strange as it may sound, I loved my family, and I couldn't bear to be without them. So, I prayed for God to help me while I tried to avoid situations. I didn't know what else to do.

I remember being home alone one day when I saw my dad approaching the house. We had two doors to our home, but they were both on the front, so there was no way to escape without being seen. My brother and I shared a bathroom that no one else used much. The door to that bathroom opened into the hallway, which was in direct sight of our living room and the chair in which my dad always sat. When I saw my dad coming toward the house this day, that bathroom was the only *safe* place I could think to go to avoid him. I felt trapped. I sat in the bathtub with the shower curtain pulled and the door closed in the dark for what seemed like hours. I was so afraid to move or to even breathe too loud, thinking he would find me and then abuse me more. I never told anyone about that day. How could I?

Finally, one day, my mom called me to her bedroom and closed the door. She asked me what was happening. At first, I didn't know how to respond, but when all I could do was cry, too afraid to tell her, she told me that God showed her about the abuse in a

dream. From that moment on, life was never the same again. I wanted things to change, and they certainly did—for the worse.

I don't really remember the exact progression of things from that point. It was like a bad dream, and I just wanted to wake up. So, I'll tell you things as I recall them. The biggest thing I remember feeling was shame. The more people who came to know the truth, the more I felt that way. I don't understand why there is so much shame attached to the person who is abused, but there is, even though they are a victim.

Not knowing what to do, my mom went to my school counselor for direction. Now, mind you, I was a freshman in high school. She also confided in our pastor and in her best friend, who was the mother of my best friend. So, everywhere I went, I felt like I had a scarlet letter on my chest. I was more scared and lonelier by the day, feeling more and more like the lonesome loser. I couldn't talk to anyone. How do you tell people something so horrible, especially when it made you feel so dirty inside?

Somehow, the "powers that be" directed my mom to Child Care Services (then just called Social Services). She and I would go there in secret so my dad and siblings wouldn't know. I remember the pain, the shame, the extreme anger, and the hurt. Here, the people asked me all kinds of questions. All I wanted to do was scream. I remember sitting in a dark, dingy office and being grilled for information. I felt like I had committed some crime, as if being abused somehow made me weak or dirty or crazy. I felt like these

people were all looking at me with disgust, and I just wanted to die.

Why was this happening to me? What did I do to deserve this? And why did they want me to give them all of the horrid details? I hated them. I hated life! I just wanted to forget. I couldn't go anywhere to escape this thing. What was worse, none of my friends knew, nor did I want them to, but I had to live everyday life pretending everything was fine.

One day, it all came to the breaking point. Until then, my dad didn't know the truth was out. This is what I refer to as the darkest, scariest night of my life—and the loneliest by far. The strange thing about the mind: sometimes the things we want to recall flee us while the things we want to forget torment us, like that night. The way I remember it, my grandparents (Gram and Pop) and my aunt came from Maryland to be with my mom, and they sat in the kitchen waiting. My brothers and sister were sent to a friend's house a few miles away so they wouldn't have to witness the scene. My dad sat in his chair watching the evening news, unaware that something was brewing, that his life was on the verge of change. I paced on the front porch, so afraid as I waited for what I was told would come.

I don't recall the exact date or even the time of year. My guess is that it was the fall of 1981 because I was a freshman and because the nights were cool and darkness set in early. As the sheriff's car turned into our driveway, I felt this sinking fear, like the blood all drained from my body. I wanted to be anywhere but there.

The social worker and the sheriff came to our door and asked for my dad to step outside. When we were all there on the front porch, they began to tell my dad about the allegations against him and that I was being removed from the home. I still remember the hurt in his eyes when he looked at me and asked me to tell the others that it wasn't true. It was almost like he couldn't believe himself what he had done. I also remember telling him that I couldn't. Then, for the only time in my life that I can ever recall, I turned to my mom, clung to her, and cried.

Next, as if I was the one who had committed a crime, I was escorted to the sheriff's car, put in the backseat, and driven off into the night. I didn't know where I was going, when I would return, or when I would ever see my family again. As time would tell, it was a home that I would never go back to, as nothing would ever be the same.

As we drove away, I was left alone to deal with all of these emotions and fears. Sure, the sheriff and the social worker were there, but it was as if they forgot about me; they were just doing their job. They talked and laughed and never even spoke to me. I know these agencies exist to protect the child, and I know their motives are good, but sometimes, behind all the red tape, they lose sight of the fact that a hurting child is involved, like that night. Let me just interject here; that was my perception, and borrowing from the words of a co-worker, perception is not necessarily reality. I don't know. Maybe it was hard for them to deal with, and they just detached themselves to make it easier.

TERRY L. SELLERS

What I do know and remember is that I was scared and I felt alone.

We drove for what seemed like hours with me constantly looking back to see if anyone was following us. It was pitch black, which added to my fears. Eventually, we came to some house. It was a foster home, and I was taken inside and left there with complete strangers. The people were excited and smiling and wanted to know all about me. They were nice enough, but they didn't seem to get it. I didn't want to be there. I just wanted my life back, before all of this started. My world was turned upside down, and the last thing I wanted to do was share the specifics with a bunch of strangers or to pretend that all was well.

Finally, I was sent to bed. I was put in bed with two younger children who were siblings and who were already asleep. They too were foster children. As I lay there, sleep would not come. My life was this big question mark. I was so scared, and all I could do was cry. I had no one to hold me and no one to tell me things were going to be all right. My heart was broken, and I couldn't see past the darkness of that moment. Sometime during the night, the strangest thing happened. The little girl beside me turned to me; hugged me; said "I love you"; and then rolled back over and was fast asleep again. I don't recall seeing that little girl ever again. That was the last thing I remember about that night but something that never left my mind.

LOVE DON'T
LIVE HERE ANYMORE

You abandoned me
Love don't live here anymore
Just a vacancy
Love don't live here anymore
When you lived inside of me
There was nothing I could conceive
That you wouldn't do for me
Trouble seemed so far away
You changed that right away, baby
Love don't live here anymore
Just emptiness and memories
Of what we had before
You went away
Found another place to stay, another home
In the windmills of my eyes
Everyone can see the loneliness inside of me
Why'd ya have to go away
Don't you know I miss you so and need your love

—Miles Gregory

Music is an outburst of the soul.

—Frederick Delius

Eventually, I went back home. Well, it was the same house, but there was no more *home*. I was only in the foster system for a few weeks, and once it was deemed safe, I was allowed to return. My dad was no longer there. He had been in jail for a while, and by the time I returned, there was a restraining order against him for my protection. I don't know exactly when Madonna came out with the song "Love Don't Live Here Anymore," but I do remember sitting alone and singing it often. It had become my new soul's song. Of course, that was the liar again. I felt abandoned, left with the emptiness and memories of what once was.

My life was supposed to return to normal. In reality, the nightmare continued. I remember the day I had to go for the court hearing to see what my fate and my dad's fate would be. The trial wasn't really inside the courtroom that day. It began long before, and it continued long afterward. I felt like I was the accused. The judge wasn't sitting on his bench, wearing a long, black robe, wielding a gavel. There were many judges. Some called themselves family, some friends.

Some relatives from my dad's family were there that day, and they looked at me like I was evil and acted as if they were disgusted with me. It really hurt. Again, I don't blame them. I know they didn't want to believe things either, but I didn't ask for this, nor did I want it. I even remember years later how my own brother told me that I was a liar and that I was the one who tore our family apart. What an awful thing for a child to bear.

TERRY L. SELLERS

The sentence from the court for me that day was to be sent to a children's home. The sentence from others was judgment and condemnation. Before I was sent away, I had to endure a battery of psychiatric evaluations, as if being abused implied that I was now crazy, or at the very least unstable.

I underwent IQ tests and mental evaluations. A few of these stick out in my mind from that time, like a bad dream. First was the inkblot test (Rorschach test). If you've never seen nor experienced it, a person holds up board after board with a big blotch of ink on each one. Then they ask you what you see or how it makes you feel. All I could see was anger. I felt like a volcano that was about to explode. Why were they doing this to me? I literally hated everyone attached to this. I know hate is a strong word, but at the time, it was the only accurate descriptive I had.

Aside from the inkblot test, there were pages of questions. I even remember having the same questions asked over and over and sometimes in slightly different forms. I thought to myself, *They must really think I'm crazy,* so I would answer them all differently. That didn't really help my cause. I also had to go sit with a counselor several times a week, and I was supposed to share with her how I felt. Yeah right. At times, others would be behind a two-way mirror, evaluating my every response and my body language. I was so angry. Why was this happening? When would it end?

In the middle of it all, my mom wanted to try to reconcile her marriage and her home. As part of his sentence, my dad had to attend AA meetings, so my mom would make us kids go to the family meetings to

show our support. Can you imagine? I was treated like a criminal of sorts. I was sent before the courts. I had to go through mental evaluations and counseling, and now I was expected to go to these meetings so my dad could return home as if nothing ever happened.

As fate would have it, I finally got sent to the children's home. Here, I received private schooling. I had to undergo individual counseling as well as group counseling. I never considered myself to be an exceptionally brilliant person, but I soon figured out that I had to play the game. And play I did. I became a master at saying the right things, the things I knew the counselor wanted to hear and the things that would shorten my sentence, allowing me to return home. In reality, I felt more unloved, more like a loser, and lonelier than ever. Some songs never leave us.

During that summer, my parents finally gave up on reconciliation, and they legally separated. My dad began seeing another woman and lived with her. My older brother moved in with our dad's sister while my younger brother and sister were sent to live with Gram and Pop in Baltimore for the summer. My family of six was now under five different roofs. As for me, life in the children's home wasn't all bad. People there didn't seem to accuse or judge me. I wasn't seen as the wrongdoer, but as the victim that I was. I formed strong bonds with the other children, and I became their leader so to speak, by their proclamation. They even began to call me Queen Bee, which still makes me laugh.

This was new for me. Most of my life, I had only heard the negative aspects of who I was. Up to that

TERRY L. SELLERS

point, I don't ever recall feeling special, but I felt it here. How strange to be among strangers yet have a sense of belonging? Don't get me wrong. I had family who loved me and who I loved very much, and I had some great friends, but I still never felt *special*. In all of this, I began to remember my prayers, my pleas for God to take me out of my home, away from the abuse, and I realized that this was an answered prayer.

In just under six months, I was released to go back home. I never considered myself a good actress, but I had managed to fool the system. I had the courts convinced that I had worked through all of the emotional garbage. In reality, the emotions were all locked safely away where no one could see. I mean, let's get real. How do you just get over something like that, and in only six months? I still had hate, anger, bitterness, shame, and worthlessness—all eating away at me. Looking back now, this whole deception wasn't just to the ones around me, but I deceived myself. More accurately, the liar was hard at work and we all were blinded to him. I put up walls of protection to keep others out so that I would never be hurt again, and there I lived for years to come, the hurt inside, everyone else outside, from a distance. Maybe that's why love didn't live there anymore, why I related to that song.

When I went back home, it was now me, my mom, and my younger brother and sister. I was a sophomore in high school. Things were okay on the surface, but I still felt the shame and judgment. There were such rumors around school that I had been raped, that I was pregnant, and that I went away to have my baby or some form of this rumor. None of that was true,

but in the minds of the believers, it all was. Everyday life was a struggle, but I kept playing the game, and I pretended not to care, all the while building my walls of protection higher and higher.

Soon, life took another turn. With the separation of my parents now legal, there was no longer a place to call home. In the separation agreement, everything was sold. My parents split the assets, counted their losses, and moved on. My younger siblings, my mom, and I were now moving to Baltimore where my mom's family lived. My older brother still lived with our aunt, and my dad still lived with some woman. Love truly didn't live there—at my childhood address—anymore, nor would it ever again for the Sellers family.

TERRY L. SELLERS

KYRIE

The wind blows hard against this mountainside
Across the sea into my soul
It reaches in to where I cannot hide
Setting my feet upon this road
My heart is old it holds my memories
This heart it burns a gem like flame
Somewhere between the soul and soft machine
Is where I find myself again
Kyrie, eleison, down the road that I must travel
Kyrie, eleison, through the darkness of the night
Kyrie, eleison, where I go you will follow
Kyrie, eleison, on a highway in the light
When I was young I dreamed of growing old
Of what my life would mean to me
Would I have traveled down my chosen road
Or only wish that I could be

—Richard Page, Steve George, and John Lang

You are the music, while the music lasts.

—T. S. Eliot

With the move to Baltimore, I was now in my third high school that year. (I had started back to public school before leaving the children's home.) My grandparents had a small rental home behind their house, and my mom, brother, and sister lived there. I stayed in an upstairs room with Gram and Pop because the other house was *too small*. By now, a new feeling was starting to take hold in my life called rejection. It seemed that I was always the one separated from the rest of the family. There had to be a reason why, and it had to be me. I was only fifteen, and I was such a mess inside.

Life seemed like a constant whirlwind. I was so good at pretending that I was okay; I think everyone believed it. My problems seemed to loom before me, yet it seemed no one else cared or even realized it. Again, that was just my perception, not reality. It probably had more to do with the walls I had built than anything else and of course, the liar. I had a very loving, supportive family on my mom's side. My mom was too busy trying to hold everything together to really see me. Again, I don't fault her. I had always felt like she had failed me. It wasn't until later in life that I realized all the ways I had failed her. My focus was on me, so I didn't see her pain, and I'm sure it was the same with her.

As a result, the chasm between us was only growing. Deep down, I felt like she blamed me for everything. (By now, you should recognize the liar, too.)

TERRY L. SELLERS

Whether that was true or not, I don't know. What I do know is that I started to foster resentment toward her. I felt like screaming, but there was no one to hear me. I felt like running, but there was no place to run. I felt like dying, yet I wanted to live. More and more, I would pray. It seemed that God was the only one I could be real with. I guess that's why the song of my soul for this chapter in my life was "Kyrie." Kyrie eleison is Greek for "Lord, have mercy." Even though I felt alone, I knew deep in my heart that God was there with me.

I just wanted life to get back to normal, whatever normal was. My mom was always telling me that I couldn't do anything right, even as a child. I guess that's why I began to try to win approval in the things that I did. My grades were improving, and I was on the basketball team. But it didn't matter how much I tried; nothing could change the way I felt inside, and nothing seemed to change how my mom looked at me. I just kept stifling those emotions and I forged ahead. I didn't really know who I was anymore.

There was a monster growing inside of me. I only felt like more of a loser, a nobody, with each passing day. I couldn't look people in the eyes, and I wouldn't speak unless spoken to. After all, I felt invisible. I craved love. My dear, sweet Gram was the only person who seemed to see me, and she loved me in the only way she knew how. She was just there. I never talked about things to her, but I knew she understood. She spent time with me and made me laugh when all I really wanted to do was cry. I'm so thankful to God for my grandparents and for their presence in my life.

Life went on and, well, "Kyrie, eleison, down the road that I must travel..." As it turns out, Daddy convinced Mama to give him another chance and move back to North Carolina. He rented a mobile home, came to Maryland to get us and back we went. This was my fourth move that school year.

This really fueled my anger and resentment toward my mom more. I couldn't believe that she would put me back in a home with my dad. He was still an alcoholic, and needless to say, things didn't work out. When it finally fell apart this time, my dad kicked us out in the cold, pouring rain. We had nothing. We had no money. We had nowhere to go. Not knowing where else to turn and I guess too embarrassed to go back to her parents, my mom went to her church for help.

She and my siblings went to live in a house that a church member provided. I guess it wasn't big enough either because I was sent to live with the new pastor and his family. He had three girls my age, but they were all strangers to me at the time. Again, I was separated from the rest of the family. I wondered if the sight of me repulsed my mom. No worries, I had my constant friends *loneliness* and *rejection* to keep me company.

Eventually, we got an apartment in government housing, and the four of us were back under one roof. Looking back, I see God even in this, as it was a brand new apartment; we were the first tenants in an end unit town home, and it was nice. Around this same time, my older brother married a woman with three children. Our family began to change in a positive way, and I was now an aunt to Casey, Kyle, and Alexandria.

TERRY L. SELLERS

Life began to settle down some. My dad lived nearby with his girlfriend but remained a part of our lives. We were made to go spend time with him. The others wanted to go but not me. I began even harder to try to get my mom's approval through other things such as sports, my grades, winning contests, etc. I thought, *If I do things right, she will love me and forgive me.* I was becoming a perfectionist, but nothing seemed to work. My parents' divorce became final my senior year. Soon after that, while in an alcoholic blackout, my dad remarried, and they had a son, my baby brother, within a year.

This may sound like an account of all the bad things that happened to me, especially via my parents, but that is not the case. There was a lot of good in my parents, and there was a lot of ways that I failed them too. My dad didn't just walk away from us, even though he did what he did. He remained a part of our lives, and later, I would be glad. My mom did the best she could to raise us in a stable environment. She didn't ask for any of this either. She actually went back to college to better provide for us.

I graduated from high school in June of 1985. On July 4, 1985, just twelve days before my eighteenth birthday, I was personally introduced to alcohol while at Myrtle Beach with the pastor's kids. It soon took over my life. The only reason for me to drink was to forget my problems. I had a lot of problems, so it took a lot of alcohol. It was funny how I could even hide the addiction.

After high school, I moved out on my own. I felt like the problem was with my family and that I needed

to get away. In reality, the problem was within me. No matter where I went, it followed me. Nonetheless, I was determined to *be somebody*, so I started college. I was going to prove all the naysayers in my life wrong.

Despite my plans, my new best friend *alcohol* got along well with my constant companions, *loneliness* and *rejection*. I even began to smoke marijuana. As much as I thought I had control, I really didn't, and I soon found myself rolling pennies just to buy a pint of Crown Royal. Then I would drink the whole bottle in one night because, although I didn't really like the taste, I liked the world it took me to, away from reality and away from the pain. Only two people seemed to notice my problem. My best friend became concerned when she was visiting my home and noticed that I didn't have groceries, yet I had alcohol. My boyfriend noticed my problem when he found the bottle I kept under my driver's seat.

Before long, I was moving from place to place and going from one job to another. I eventually quit college and even walked out on a job in the middle of the night shift. I looked for meaning in relationships because that led to love, and I thought love would make things all right. That was just more of the lies I believed from yours truly, the liar. This wasn't the person I wanted to be, but I had lost control.

When the alcohol wore off, the loneliness and pain still hung around. One night, I reached the brink of desperation. I no longer wanted to live. I scraped together enough money for one last pint of liquor and, after I reached the bottom of that bottle, my courage was strong. I got in my car with the intent to die. That

TERRY L. SELLERS

way, no one would know. It would look like an alcohol-related death instead of suicide.

I built up my speed as fast as my little car would go; and then I steered for the trees. But that night I believe a guardian angel stepped in. To those of you who have prayed for your family members for years and think that God has forgotten or ignored you, don't believe the liar. I am convinced that all the prayers my mom, Gram and others had prayed over me for years intervened at that moment. All I know is that I tried to steer off of the road, but I felt a force that I couldn't reckon with take the steering wheel and bring me back onto the road. When it was over, I was at a loss. I could never tell anyone what had happened. First, I knew no one would ever believe me, and, second, I didn't want anyone to know that I tried to or even wanted to commit suicide. That's what cowards do, and I didn't want to be known as a coward.

This is not something that I'm proud of or that I share easily. However, I do know what hopelessness looks like, how desperation feels. More importantly, I now know that life doesn't have to be that way; there is hope for anyone who finds themselves in that same place of despair. As Carrie Underwood says in her song, all you have to do is let "Jesus take the wheel" of your life. I can assure you, you won't be disappointed.

After that night, I knew I needed help. Maybe I didn't die in the physical realm, but inside, I was already dead. All of those walls I had erected couldn't protect me from what was on the inside. In search of change but not willing to turn to God, I turned to Uncle Sam. I joined the US Army, hoping it would take me away

from my life of heartache and pain. I began the lon-gest run of my life, away from God! Or was it to him? Kyrie, eleison, through the darkness of the night.

TERRY L. SELLERS

HERE I
GO AGAIN

No, I don't know where I'm going
But, I sure know where I've been
Hanging on the promises
In songs of yesterday
An' I've made up my mind,
I ain't wasting no more time
Here I go again
Here I go again
Tho' I keep searching for an answer,
I never seem to find what I'm looking for
Oh Lord, I pray
You give me strength to carry on,
'Cos I know what it means
To walk along the lonely street of dreams
An' here I go again on my own
Goin' down the only road I've ever known,
Like a drifter I was born to walk alone
An' I've made up my mind
I ain't wasting no more time
I'm just another heart in need of rescue,
Waiting on love's sweet charity
An' I'm gonna hold on
For the rest of my days,
'Cos I know what it means
To walk along the lonely street of dreams

—David Coverdale and Bernie Marsden

Music speaks what cannot be expressed, soothes the mind and gives it rest, heals the heart and makes it whole, flows from heaven to the soul.

—Unknown

There are very few moments that really stand out in my memory, but the day I was at the bus station leaving for the army is one of those moments. Several of my good friends came to say their good-byes—my younger siblings and my mom too. But the memory that I couldn't erase from my mind was when I looked out from the bus window just before pulling away and I saw my mom cry.

For the life of me, I didn't know why. I thought she hated me and that she didn't care, so why would she be crying? I guess that was the liar once again. If ever there was a song in my soul that defined me, one that I truly believed, this was it: "Here I go again on my own...like a drifter I was born to walk alone..." I mean, wasn't she the one that always isolated me, as if punishment for what I had done to our family? I thought the life of a loner was my fate, so why the tears?

In a way, I was running from things as hard as I could. In another way, I was fighting to survive as hard as I could. But do you want to know the funny thing about this chapter of my life? Looking back now, I realize the author or the composer, if you will, was actually God. Even when I was living such a lifestyle, I truly believe God directed my steps to join the army. I say this because it was a major turning point for me.

In the army, we were all strangers. The playing field was level. No one knew anything about the other,

TERRY L. SELLERS

and, more importantly, no one knew anything about me. People didn't judge me; they just accepted me for who I was. It was this big melting pot where everyone was needed and wanted. We became a family of sorts.

Here, my perfectionism really paid off. I wasn't told all the negative qualities about me (as one might think), but I was rewarded for the good things. Here, I began to change. I began to hold my head high for the first time, and I began to see myself in a different light. I was somebody, and I did have something to offer after all.

I guess the same force that turned my steering wheel that night was now a force turning my heart. I had always had a strong belief in God, even as a child, and I had prayed to him all of my life. I still wasn't yielding my life to God, but I began to feel him tug at my heart more and more.

The strange thing is how we often tend to believe what others think about us. Growing up, I believed the kids who called me names, the ones who constantly pointed out the bad in me. I believed the lie that I could never do anything right. *But now*, I believed the ones around me. I no longer felt like this big loser. I was becoming self-confident. I could look people in the eyes. Something was definitely changing inside of me.

Although things seemed better, I still had anger, hurt, shame, guilt, and my walls of protection. In fact, I'll never forget the day when a lot of the anger surfaced. I don't even recall what precipitated this, but I do remember being in an almost empty barracks on a beautiful summer day at Ft. Hood, Texas and feeling like I was a volcano about to explode. I shut the win-

dow and blinds to my room and turned my stereo wide open to drown out the noise as I began to just scream and cry and bang on things. This went on for more than an hour. When it was all over, strangely, I felt better. I was emotionally and physically spent, but I really felt better. I guess things had been building inside for so long and I needed that release. If you think child abuse is something that you can just get over, be glad you're not a victim.

After that day, things actually did become better. I was what I *perceived* to be happy for the first time in a long time. I had a close friendship with my roommate. We had so much fun together; we even told people we were sisters. Life was becoming the ultimate party! I was in the clubs every weekend. I dated so many guys. I had new friends, job security, money—life was good! Of course, alcohol and marijuana were still a part of my lifestyle, but now it was all for pleasure. This was different. This made it okay. I didn't seem so much like an addict now; it was justified. I now had a false sense of security.

In the middle of it all, I still felt this tugging at my heart. I tried to ignore it. One day, while home on leave from Texas, I was visiting and talking with my niece, Alex. This was another one of those moments in my life that just stood out as meaningful and unforgettable—precious!

We were at her grandmother's house. Alex was standing on the top rung of the stairs up to the porch while I was standing at the bottom, facing her so that we were looking eye to eye. She was about five years old, and she was sporting her new Texas Minnie Mouse

TERRY L. SELLERS

t-shirt that I had given her, along with a necklace of hers. It was long with polished faux stones, something apparently special to her.

Alex looked at me and said, "Aunt Terry, if I give you something, will you keep it forever?" I replied yes, not sure what was to follow. She reached up, took off her necklace, and put it around my neck. I thought it was the most precious thing. There was nothing attached to my receiving it, but it was given with such love. And, she wanted *me* to have it *forever*! It was special, priceless.

I believe that was what God was trying to do with me, except he wanted me to do the giving. He wanted me to give him my heart, hurts and all, and know that he would keep it forever. I just had to give; he would receive. In return, he would love me and keep me *forever*! How precious is that? (And yes, Ting Ding, I still have your necklace, forever!) When I joined the army, I felt like a drifter going out on my own again. Yet, there I was, thousands of miles from home, and God was still there. I just wasn't ready to give him my heart.

NEW ATTITUDE

I'm feelin' good from my head to my shoes
Know where I'm goin' and I know what to do
I tidied up my point of view
I got a new attitude
Runnin' hot, runnin' cold
I was runnin' into overload
It was extreme, ex-ex-ex-ex-ex-extreme
It took it so high, so low
So low, there was nowhere to go
Like a dream
Somehow the wires uncrossed, the tables were turned
Never knew I had such a lesson to learn
Chorus:
I'm in control, my worries are few
'Cause I've got love like I never knew
Ooh, ooh, ooh, ooh, ooh
I got a new attitude
I'm wearing a new dress (New), new hair (New)
Brand-new ideas, as a matter of fact I've changed for good
It must have been the cool night, new moon,
    new slight change
More than to figure But I feel like I should, yes
Somehow the wires uncrossed, the tables were turned
Never knew I had such a lesson to learn

—Bunny Hull, Jon Gilutin, and Sharon T. Robinson

Music is an outburst of the soul.

—Frederick Delius

Although my complete military commitment was eight years, my active duty enlistment was only for two years. It was a special enlistment in which I was offered more college money, dubbed the college fund, and less active duty time as an incentive to go into a specific job that wasn't too attractive to potential recruits. It worked for me because it was only a two-year commitment. Although I loved my country and took my oath seriously, I didn't want to be in the military for that long if I didn't like it.

When I was discharged from the army and I returned to my hometown, I truly had a new attitude. At any given point in my life, I always had a song to sing, but this song, "I've Got a New Attitude," resonated how I now felt, and I wanted people to know. I was back, and I was better. Look at me now!

Once my self-perspective changed, it also changed how others perceived me. People were constantly telling me that I was different. In a way, I was. I was more confident, and I was more determined to make it. But, in reality, I was still the same person I had always been on the inside, the person few people cared to know before. Perhaps some of that was due to my walls of protection that were still up and stronger than ever, but some of it was due to their judgments of me. The only real difference now was that I saw myself differently, and I began to live it out.

Now that I was home, I had a plan, a career goal in mind, and I started pursuing it. I was back living

TERRY L. SELLERS

with my mom. My younger brother was still at home too. My sister was now married and had a beautiful baby girl, another new purpose for me. I was rekindling old friendships and dating different guys. The partying I started in the army continued. My plan was to attend the local community college while I applied to and waited for acceptance to a college that offered my career choice.

Even though life seemed different, deep inside, I wasn't. Deep inside, there was still a lot of hurt; there was still a lot of pain; there was still a lot of anger. And even though I seemed to be surrounded by friends, deep inside, I was still lonely. Maybe I did have a new dress, new shoes, new attitude, but those were only on the surface, changing only the outside. You can dress up all you want, but it has no bearing on the matters of the heart. That change comes at a greater price.

Regardless, before long, my plan was in motion, and I was back in college. This time it was different. This time I really wanted to be there, and my grades reflected my dedication. For the first time in my life, I found that I wasn't so dumb after all. All I had to do was study and apply myself. I actually began to excel, and my sense of self grew stronger and stronger. In fact, I was asked to tutor college algebra, and I did. Classmates actually sought me out for help.

Looking back now, I realize that was pride, and it was a dangerous place to be. Doesn't the Bible say in Proverbs 16:18 that pride goes before destruction? Trust me, it does, but don't just take my word; look it up for yourself. I think that verse holds true for everyone, Christian or not. I began to feel like I had control

of my life and that I was actually the one changing it for the better. Yes, we do have to make wise choices. We are ultimately responsible for the choices we make and the consequences of those choices, but there are other forces or events that also affect us. Pride was certainly a negative force for me.

Pride left me feeling in control to the point that I didn't *need* God and I had no time for him. Even though I had always felt God's tug at my heart, I now thought he couldn't love me too much. If he did, why had he allowed all the hurt, the pain, and the abuse? Why had he allowed my family to fall apart and to suffer so much? Didn't he have the power to stop it all? No. I didn't need a God like that.

There was another prevailing thought in my mind: I was still young. I could be a Christian when I was older, when I had nothing else to do. If you want to talk about a lie straight from the liar, this was certainly one. I knew enough of the Bible to know that it clearly says I wasn't promised tomorrow. In 2 Corinthians 6:2, the Bible says that *now* is the day of salvation, and Luke 12:40 says that the Son of man will come at an hour when you do not expect him. Even though I wasn't serving God, he was clearly at work in me. I mean, why would I even think about such things? That wasn't something the liar wanted me to dwell or meditate on. I truly believed in God and that there was (is) a heaven and a hell. I just didn't want to worry about it right now. I would have time later. Unfortunately, I believed that I didn't need God right now, if ever.

I was young. Life was finally *good*. I was going to enjoy my life, and live it up while I still could. You see,

my pride told me that I had it all figured out. I was raised in the church, and I knew what the Bible taught. If God came back before I got old, grew tired of my selfish living, and decided to live for him, or if I missed the rapture then I still had another chance, one last hope. I knew all about the tribulation and the mark of the beast and all that Revelation foretells. Therefore, I would know not to take the mark of the beast—which is 666—and that I could make it into heaven in the end because I knew to give my heart to God then.

Maybe I'm the only one who has ever thought these things and who has actually believed them, but I was standing on lies. Jeremiah 12:5 says, "If you have raced with men on foot and they have worn you out, how can you compete with horses? If you stumble in safe country, how will you manage in the thickets by the Jordan?" I think it's safe to equate my life at this point as racing on foot with men, in safe country. And it's safe to equate life after the rapture, during the tribulation, as competing with horses in the thickets by the Jordan. Would I truly be able to finally give my life to God in the tribulation and not give in to the antichrist and the mark of the beast, assuming I even survived until the end? I think not. These were just more thoughts from the liar that I believed and stood on.

After all of this, I still had one last false hope, just in case all else failed or if life threw me another curveball. What if I didn't grow old, turning to God then, or what if I didn't actually miss the rapture and live through the tribulation, turning to God then? Suppose I actually got in an accident or someone else took my life? My thought was that I could call on God with my last dying breath if need be, and he would hear me because I had always been taught that God was merciful and forgiving. In this scenario, I could slide into heaven just in the nick of time.

This was the place I was now at. I had my *get to heaven* back-up plan while I lived however I chose. I was walking tall with a sense of pride. I certainly had a new attitude, but it was all built on lies. I was telling myself all the reasons I didn't need God right now or why I should wait to turn to God when I was older, and I was foolish enough to believe them. That's when life did throw me another curve, when my soul's song really did change, and I had yet another new attitude.

TERRY L. SELLERS

Amazing Grace

Amazing grace, how sweet the sound
That saved a wretch like me
I once was lost but now I'm found
Was blind but now I see
Twas grace that taught my heart to fear
And grace my fears relieved
How precious did that grace appear
The hour I first believed
Through many dangers, toils and snares
I have already come
Tis grace hath brought me safe thus far
And grace will lead me home
When we've been there ten thousand years
Bright shining as the sun
We've no less days to sing God's praise
Than when we first begun

—John Newton

When the music changes, so does the dance.

—African Proverb

If I had to name a pivotal point in my life, it would be the military. If I had to name a life-changing event for me, just one day in my life, it would have to be May 1, 1990. If I had to name the life-changer, it was and still is, without a doubt, God!

On May 1, 1990, God proved to me that I was not promised tomorrow. I wasn't even promised my next breath, and on this day, I was just a few breaths away from hell. That's when God stepped in with his *amazing grace*. On this day, I was in an automobile accident that almost took my life. I can honestly say that during the times of consciousness, not once did I think of God, despite all of my theories. My life did not flash before my eyes. I did not see some light.

May 1, 1990 was a typical Tuesday for me. I got up, did my morning routine, and went off to classes at the local junior college where I attended. My last class was over at 10:30 a.m. I had plans to meet another classmate, and off we went to Ocean Isle Beach where we met up with two other friends. It was a beautiful day to be alive, especially at the beach. The four of us spent the next several hours swimming, sunning, drinking, and a few other less virtuous things. When it was time to start back toward home, we all decided to meet up again for a cookout in a few hours to continue our party.

I went home to shower. One of the others came by to pick me up. The plan was for us to pick up her child from her parents' house, and then we would go on to

TERRY L. SELLERS

the cookout. Aside from the fact that we had both had too much alcohol to be driving, we were now running late to pick up her child, so we were also speeding. We came to a part of the road that helped define the word *curvy*. It was a single-lane, country road that went out of one sharp curve right into another one in the opposite direction. As we entered the second curve, it was at this point that we both realized we were going to wreck. Things became a little weird, for lack of a better word, almost twilight zone like.

I recall looking over to my friend and saying, "We're going to wreck, aren't we?" and I recall her looking back at me, laughing, and saying "yes." The really weird part is that I could see but I couldn't actually hear. And when I say she laughed, it wasn't really her that I saw. I saw what I perceived to be Satan, and I then heard him mockingly say the words, "You're going to die," as she laughed. Immediately afterward, I felt such peace as I heard the words, "No, you're not," none of which was actually audible.

After that, I remember us skidding out of control, and then I was thrown into the floor of the truck. Everything went black. Now, my hearing was acute, but I could no longer see anything. I could hear the sound of metal bending and scraping, the sound of glass breaking and of tires squealing. Then, I felt and heard the impact of us hitting something really hard. Later, this would prove to be a tree that we hit so hard it was uprooted.

From that moment on, the story had to be pieced together by the state highway patrol officers who later told us what presumably happened, as I was uncon-

scious at that point. Apparently, after the impact, we began to roll and flip, with my body hanging halfway out of the truck. I was stuck, and now the truck was sliding down the road with me between the road and the truck. My back was against the pavement and was being ripped apart. With the next flip of the truck, I was thrown free from the vehicle.

The next thing I remember is hearing my friend calling my name. It was over. She was alive, but she couldn't find me. The truck had landed off of the road on the driver's side. The only glass broken out was the passenger's side window, which was apparently where I was hanging out as the truck slid down the road and also the window she crawled out of moments later. When I heard her calling for me, I said, "I'm here," not really knowing where here was.

She kept calling, and I told her that something was on my foot. As soon as I got it off, I would get up and come to her. I couldn't see, but I do remember digging my foot down into the dirt to free it. Once I did free my foot, I told her that I was going to get up. At that moment, she found me and, in a nervous laugh, said, "No, you're not. The truck is on top of you." She was right. I just hadn't realized it. The truck had landed on the right side of my body. I couldn't move, and I was drifting in and out of consciousness. She went to the road and began to flag down a car that was approaching.

Several cars stopped. One was a nurse on her way to work at the hospital. In fact, all that stopped were women. These women actually got around the truck and lifted it up enough so one of them could slide

me out. This was before cell phones, so I don't know how an ambulance was summoned or even how long it took.

My next recollection was that of me being on a stretcher and lifted into the ambulance with my friend by my side. I remember being too afraid to close my eyes again, thinking that I might die. I couldn't control that, but I can tell you this: not even once did I think of God and calling out to him. Had I left earth that night, my theories of how I would slide into heaven by the skin of my teeth would have all been shattered as I landed in hell for eternity. Even at the hospital, I still didn't think of God, yet all the while, I thought I was dying.

The doctor on call that evening stood over me and literally cried as he told me how lucky I was just to be alive. I later learned that he had recently lost his only son in an automobile accident. He was only sixteen. Still, I had no thought of God. News traveled fast, and apparently, the waiting room was filled with people who cared about my friend and me. Most of my family was there. My sister and another friend, who was like an older sister to me, stood by my side as I screamed and cried out in pain while the medical staff accessed my injuries and began to pick glass and debris out of my skin. It was one of the worse pains I ever remember.

I was truly fortunate just to be alive, as my doctor had stated. In the end, my injuries were not life-threatening. My liver was lacerated, but it could heal itself. I had some broken bones in my right ankle and shoulder and fractures in my spine but nothing critical.

I had a few cuts on my face and elsewhere but nothing that needed stitches. My back and right arm were raw, with little skin left in areas. I did need stitches on my arm but couldn't get them due to the injuries there. Later, I was also found to have nerve damage in my right eye and what would become permanent nerve damage in my right arm.

I spent the next ten days in the hospital. The pain was unreal, and I especially hated it when the nurse came in to change the bandages on my back. They would just jerk the bandage—it covered my entire back—but it was the best way to do it, in one, quick motion. It was like ripping open my flesh again each time. I couldn't help but cry out in agony.

Besides the fact that my injuries weren't more substantial, I had tremendous support. My room was constantly filled with family and friends. Cards and flowers poured in. I was so blessed. All of my life, the liar had told me that no one really cared about me, but here was the proof. In fact, there was someone with me twenty-four hours a day. Finally, by the eighth night, I was so tired that I actually asked everyone to leave so I could rest.

So far, I had not gotten out of bed. I wasn't able to. On this particular night, as luck would have it with me being alone, the nurse came in and pulled out my catheter. Later, I had to use the rest room, which meant that I had to get out of bed and walk. I hadn't done that for over a week, and it wasn't until that moment that a few realities started to set in. I couldn't use my right arm at all. My nurse call button and the phone were both on the right side of the bed, just out of reach, and none of

TERRY L. SELLERS

the staff came in to check on me. I was so weak that it took me over an hour just to get out of bed.

When I finally stood up, I used my IV pole as a crutch and took a few steps over to the sink and mirror. For the first time in eight days, I saw myself, and it was then that I finally thought of God, and I began to cry. One look in the mirror told me that God had truly spared my life. I then remembered the voices I had heard on May 1, the night of the accident, but more specifically the voice that said, "No, you're not." Suddenly, I realized that had been the voice of God. Once again, I was a product of prayer and God's grace.

All of the events of that fateful day and night started flooding my memory, and I became so depressed and lonely. Thankfully, by early morning, my room was already filled with people. A good friend from high school had stopped by prior to going to work. She assisted me as she held the phone to my ear while my uncle, a pastor in Baltimore, called to tell me that he, his son, and my Gram were coming to see me. His reason: because God told him to come. Next, my friend again held the phone as my aunt in California had called. She told me how she was at church the night before when a lady she didn't even know came to her. The lady said that God had revealed to her that she had a niece in the hospital in North Carolina who needed a *love visit*. My aunt called to say that she couldn't come to North Carolina but she did love me.

This may all sound a little strange to you, but for me, God was proving that he was not only alive and real but that he did know and care about me. After my family arrived from Maryland and visited with me for a while, my uncle asked to be alone with me.

He told me that he had the same dream three nights in a row when God told him to get out of bed and drive to North Carolina to tell me. He dreamed that it was meant for me to die that night but that God had spared my life. That morning of May 9, 1990, I finally stopped running, and I gave my life to God. It truly was his *amazing grace* that spared a wretch like me, giving me one more chance at life. My eyes were partially unveiled to Satan and all of his lies that had caused me to live in defeat for so long. This was a song I could sing with conviction and so different than all the songs before. "How sweet the sound." How could I say no to God now?

THE LIGHTHOUSE

There's a lighthouse on a hillside
That overlooks life's sea
When I'm tossed it sends out a light
That I might see
And the light that shines in darkness now
Will safely lead me o're
If it wasn't for the lighthouse
My ship would be no more.
And I thank God for the lighthouse
I owe my life to Him
For Jesus is the lighthouse
And from the rocks of sin
He has shown a light around me
That I could clearly see
If it wasn't for the lighthouse
Where would this ship be?
Everybody that lives around us says tear
    that lighthouse down
The big ships don't sail this way anymore
There's no use in it standing 'round
But then my mind goes back to that stormy night
When just in time I saw the light
And the light from that old lighthouse
That stands up there on a hill.

—Ronnie Hinson

Alas for those that never sing, But die with all their music in them!

—Oliver Wendell Holmes

When I was discharged from the army, I returned home with a new attitude. And even though my soul's song was now joyous compared to ones before, my heart was still the same: sinful and dirty. But on the evening of May 11, when I was discharged from the hospital, I was not the same person who had been admitted. I was now a new creation in Christ. I had a heart transplant, and the doctors didn't even realize it. I now had a new song in my soul, one of real joy. Not only was the song new, the beat was different, better!

Most people who really know me also know that I love lighthouses. But what they probably don't know is that this song, "The Lighthouse," is the whole reason why. I look at a lighthouse as symbolic of God, a *strong tower* as described many times in the book of Psalms. Proverbs 18:10 says that just his *name* is a strong tower; the righteous run to it and are safe. God is a refuge from the storm, sending out his light to the soul that is troubled and lost. That was me, but now, King Jesus is *my lighthouse.*

My road to recovery was long and hard. My family, especially my sister, had to help bathe me, dress me, and feed me, among other things in the first few weeks. My younger brother even helped me put on my shoes and got me out of the house when I needed a change of scenery. (Ah, the love of family.) My mom drove me from one appointment to the next. I spent the next year

TERRY L. SELLERS

and a half out of work and between doctor offices and physical therapy.

One of the first things I had to do in therapy was to pick pennies up off of a table. It may sound crazy, but I couldn't do that in the beginning due to the nerve damage in my arm. Occasionally, while walking, my left leg would just give out, and I would fall. At night, I would have nightmares, if I was able to sleep at all. Often while driving, I would have flashbacks of the accident, and I would have to pull off of the road. For a long time, if I heard an ambulance, I would become fearful and begin to shake uncontrollably, although I never told anyone about this.

I did start back to college. How I managed that between all of the therapy and doctor appointments was a miracle in itself. Eventually, my doctors told me there was nothing else that could be done, that I was going to live the rest of my life in pain. They were pretty much right about that. They wanted me to put my life on hold and go live in a pain clinic at UNC Hospital in Chapel Hill for three months to learn how to live with and how to manage the pain. I decided to trust God in that area, declining to go, and I was finally released from medical care, just after I had surgery on my right hand due to carpel tunnel sustained from the accident.

During all of this, I was not just back in church, but I was striving to live a life worthy of the second chance I had been given. I sang in the young adult choir. (It was the "Joyful Noise Choir" thanks to me.) I taught the kindergarten Sunday school class, and I also co-taught the Wednesday night children's pro-

gram. In all of that, I knew there was something missing, something I just wasn't getting. I began to pray and ask God to take me to a place where I could grow spiritually. I knew I would soon be moving to further my education, but I also desired to learn more about God and the Bible.

I had applied to several colleges in the state of North Carolina that offered my chosen career choice. In the spring of 1992, I graduated from the local junior college with all the prerequisites needed to continue my pursuit—and with two associate's degrees. I was soon informed that I was accepted by two colleges; however, God opened the door for me elsewhere. In April of that year, out of over four hundred applicants with more than 240 of us having met all requirements, I was chosen to be one of only thirty-one students to be accepted into the program at a third college.

This may not seem like a big deal, but hindsight is 20/20. Looking back, I now know that God's hand was the deciding factor. I was praying in earnest to know him more, and he took me to a church in Greenville, North Carolina, where he would begin to do that. It just so happened to also be the town where the college was, a college I would not have even applied to were it not for the friendship I had developed with my physical therapist.

When I was accepted by this third college in Greenville, I called information (this was before the day of google.com) to find a listing for a Church of God in the area, the denomination I had been raised in. I was told there were none, so I then asked for a listing of Assemblies of God churches in the area. After

TERRY L. SELLERS

I moved to Greenville and I had attended the local Assembly of God church for a while, I found out that I was misinformed. Not only were there three Churches of God in Greenville, one was only a mile from my new residence. The Bible says in Proverbs 3:5–6 to "Trust in the Lord with all of your heart and lean not on your own understanding; in all of your ways acknowledge him, and he will [direct your steps]" (my paraphrase). That's just what he was doing in my life, directing my steps as I turned to him, just as he directed me to this church.

Even though I knew I was where I belonged, I couldn't deny that things were still a struggle for me. My course load was heavy and required a lot of my time. Also, for the first time, I was completely on my own. I lived two and a half hours from family and friends, and I didn't really know anyone in Greenville. I was supposed to have a friend living with me as my roommate and classmate, but that fell through at the last minute. She changed her mind, and, although I was upset then, I later saw God in even that.

But as a result, I was now responsible for all of the bills instead of just half that I had planned on: the rent, lights, water, food, cable, phone, plus car care, and my education—you know how it works. Everything! I had scholarships, grants, loans, the GI Bill with the college fund, and I did college work-study. I wasn't the best at money management, and with all of that, it still wasn't enough to always pay the bills. My faith began to grow in a different area as I was learning to trust that God would supply my every need according to Philippians 4:19. No matter what, I was faithful in

my giving, as commanded in Malachi 3:10 where God tells us to bring *all* of our tithes and offerings into the storehouse (the church). In fact, it is the only place in the Bible where God tells us to test him and see if he won't do what he says.

I developed some quick and strong friendships with some of my classmates. We spent so much time together between classes, clinical rotations and studying together that we became like family. I recall sitting with them at lunch on a particular day when one friend asked if any of us were interested in going downtown that night, to a club. It was ladies' night, and the cover charge was only one dollar. I replied no. I stated that I no longer frequented bars and that I also only had three cents in my bank account, not even enough for the cover charge. They all laughed, thinking I was joking, but had they noticed the essence of my lunch for the third day now, they would have seen that it consisted of saltine crackers with a thin layer of peanut butter washed down by water.

I don't know why finances were the area God first began to teach me in, but it was. When you're tired of eating peanut butter crackers and drinking water because you're broke, giving tithes and offerings to the church is difficult. Obedience isn't always easy. I remember during that time I had a daily scripture calendar, and one of my verses was Matthew 6:25–34. Verses 31–33 read like this: "So do not worry, saying, 'What shall we eat?' or 'What shall we drink?' ... your heavenly Father knows that you need them. But seek first his kingdom and his righteousness, and all these things will be given to you as well."

TERRY L. SELLERS

That following Sunday at church, a message was spoken that said, "I am your God, and I will meet your financial needs." How timely. I just needed to believe and to be faithful to give, even when in need myself. Do you want to talk about stretching my faith? That very same day, I felt like God was compelling me to commit to twenty dollars a month to sponsor a child through Metro Ministries. Phil Greenaway was speaking at church that day, telling us about this children's ministry in the ghettos of New York and the daily war zone in which the children lived.

He spoke about the tremendous needs right here in America, and now, somehow my needs seemed so insignificant. To some people, twenty dollars was a small price to pay to help better the life of a child. To me, a single college student without the financial backing of my parents, it was a lot. I had no funds to pledge, but I was obedient anyway. The words of Matthew 6 were fresh in my heart, and I knew God would somehow provide if this was his will.

Later that week, I was called into the VA counselor's office where he told me that, for the first time in seven years, my program was getting a raise. I would be getting thirty dollars more each month in my VA check. God was amazing; he provided above and beyond what he asked of me. That same week, I was told that my student loan had finally been approved, and I was given two checks for over eight hundred dollars each. Of course, it was a loan, but you couldn't tell me it wasn't God's provision. Thank God for the peanut butter and cracker days! Not only did God provide, but a few years later, I was blessed to spend

a month with Metro Ministries in New York, and I got to meet my sponsored child, Samantha. She and I even got to attend a Mets game together. I would also meet and adopt my second child through the program, Chad.

I can tell you story after story of God's provision for me. One Sunday after church, the singles group was having a potluck meal. I was asked to bring rolls. I only had two dollars to my name, so I was torn. I wanted to go to the meal mainly because I didn't want to spend the day alone; however, I didn't want to go empty-handed either. I knew if I bought the rolls, I wouldn't have money to put in the offering plate that night at church. It wasn't a requirement that I give an offering, just a desire I had. I was praying about this as I walked through the near-empty parking lot to the grocery story, still uncertain what to do when a dollar bill blew right up to my feet. So what? It was only a dollar. But there was no one else in sight to return it to, and now I could give in the offering *and* I could attend the meal with something to contribute to both. God saw my heart, and he supplied its desire.

Maybe that means nothing to you—a dollar, big deal. That was just one incident; here's another one. At Christmas, my church had a tree in the foyer with photo ornaments. They were of children living in the local *project* areas. On the back of each ornament was a wish for a Christmas gift. Church members were asked to take an ornament and purchase the gift listed, which was around twenty dollars for each. I went to the tree one morning and began to read the back of these when one in particular caught my attention. The

little girl in the photo had simply asked for prayer for her mother. It broke my heart, and I really wanted to sponsor her and to pray for her and her mom.

As I've mentioned before, I had no money, but I took the ornament. I told God that I would pray for the child, and I asked him to provide the money to purchase a gift. The very next person that walked into the church was a teenager. He walked up to me, put twenty dollars in my hand, and kept walking. He never said a word.

My point here is that I had learned that God would provide and no one could convince me otherwise. God doesn't always work that way, as he did for me in those earlier days, but he does always provide. Like someone recently told me, if it's God's will, it's his bill. He was teaching me not only the principal of giving but how he cares for his own.

The song inside of me was starting to come alive. I knew that God had spared my life. He was a light-house, *my lighthouse*, to my very troubled sea, and he saved me just in time, as the song says. I didn't die with the music, the song still in my heart, unsung on that fateful night of May 1, 1990. I was alive, and I was given a chance not only to sing again, but to help shed the light into someone else's life. That's exactly what I wanted to do.

UNWORTHY
OF THE BLOOD

I don't know why the sovereign King would leave
    His throne on high
And dwell here in this barren land with
    mortals such as I.
He left His home in paradise, oh why, I'll never know
But His precious blood has made me purer
    than the virgin snow.
Chorus:
Here am I so unworthy of the blood
So unworthy of the blood that set me free.
Here am I so unworthy of the blood
But yet it flowed for me.
For every time I falter and I bring the Father shame
A droplet of His precious blood then
    falls upon my name.
I'll never know the reason why this thing
    has come to be.
All I know is that He did it just for you and me.

—Jeff Ross

He put a new song in my mouth, a hymn of praise to our God.

Psalms 40:3a

I was in college in Greenville for three years, two years for my first degree in radiology and one year for a more specialized degree in medical sonography. When I moved to Greenville, I had every intention of returning home. I would soon learn that my plans and God's plan for my life were not always the same but his plan was best. I just needed to wait on and trust in him.

I learned to trust in God by spending time studying the Bible and by having personal devotions. I also learned trust through trials and experiences. To me, it isn't about a religion; this is a relationship with a living God. Just going to church won't cut it. That's like always showing up for class but never studying. Just as the teacher can't give you all you need, neither can the pastor. Eventually, you have to read the *book* and apply it, or you'll fail. The last thing that I want anyone to say about me is that I'm religious. It's so much deeper than that.

College was tough. That alone kept me on my knees in prayer because I really wanted to obtain my goal. For the most part, I had felt my life was a failure to this point. I had a need to prove to myself that I could succeed in life.

Because I *had* developed the habit of a personal devotional time, God really began to speak to me. I don't mean audibly but he spoke to me through his Word, through dreams and sermons, through other people, and even through my past. Mostly, when God

TERRY L. SELLERS

speaks to any of us, it's like this thought that defies our reasoning, but it just won't go away. And, of course, it lines up with the Bible. I'm fully convinced that we have to develop the habit of personal Bible study and prayer to learn the voice of God. Going to church and hearing sermons is great and vital, but that should be no substitute for one's own study of the Word. I know I've already mentioned this but I can't stress it enough. If you don't know what God says in his Word, how will you ever know how to combat the liar? When the storms of life come, and they will come, what will you cling to? How will you know God's voice?

I'll admit I struggled with my Bible reading at first. I still struggle some from time to time. I recall visiting with my Gram one week and sharing my struggle with her. We were sitting on the back porch swing, and she began to share some of her life with me and how she came to know Christ. She wasn't raised in a Christian home, but when she became a Christian, she told me that she just read the Bible faithfully and asked God to give her the understanding.

She also told me that she prayed about everything, no matter how silly it seemed, like how to fix her hair. She said that God cared about the details in our lives. "If it was important to us, it was important to God," she said. Gram told me to just pray and be faithful in my Bible reading and trust that God would do the rest. And he did. He opened his Word to me in ways I never expected. He also opened my life to the world of Christian music. I found strength there in the songs that I heard. God gives us gifts to bless others, and musical talent is a gift. I, for one, am grateful to all of

the artists who use their gift for God. It has been a blessing in my life in ways unspeakable.

As time went along, I just continued to study, both my Bible and in college, living the best I could. One day, I was washing my white school uniforms and some ink got all over them. I rewashed them, and, after three times using bleach and stain removers, nothing was removing the ink. I was getting a little upset because I had to wear these uniforms to my clinical rotations and I couldn't really afford to buy new ones. Finally, I decided to pray when the thought kept coming to me, *Wash them seven times.* At first, I thought, *That's just absurd.* But then the story of the Israelites came to mind, how God had them march around the walls of Jericho seven times before the walls fell.

Absurd or not, I decided to wash them seven times, and, wouldn't you know, after the seventh wash cycle, every stain was gone off of every single uniform. You're probably thinking the same thing I was. Well, actually, you're probably thinking, *Yeah, right*, and that this is silly, but I was thinking, *Couldn't God have just done that the first time?* The answer was yes, but I guess God wanted me to learn his voice and to obey. And you're probably thinking God has bigger problems to solve than a stain on my clothes; why would he be concerned about something so trivial? I'll tell you why. It wasn't trivial to me, and just as Gram told me, it mattered to me, so it mattered to God. It's that simple, and I was learning how much God wanted to be a part of every aspect of my life.

God gave me plenty of chances to grow and to learn this simple truth. At one point in my college

TERRY L. SELLERS

career, my classes became so difficult that I was ready to quit. There were a lot of things happening in my personal life and with my family that were also vying for my time and attention. Where my family was concerned, rest assured, there was always drama. Anyway, I was struggling with a particular class, and it came to a climax one day when I had an appointment with my instructors. One of them actually told me that my chosen field wasn't for everyone and maybe I should reconsider and *just go home.* The liar was behind all of that and I admit, he had me pretty discouraged.

My response to her was, "I came here for ultrasound, and I'm not leaving until I have it." I stood strong, but in reality, I felt so defeated. If you think words aren't that important, know that she almost destroyed my career choice and future that day with her words. I remember going home afterward and just lying on my couch crying my eyes out. I told God that I couldn't do it anymore; I was ready to go back to Whiteville and admit defeat. In the middle of my pity party, I kept hearing this thought, that voice say to me, *You haven't read my Word today.* My thought or reply back was, "I know, God, but what does that have to do with this?" After the third time of this conversation with God and him interrupting my party, I finally said okay, and I picked up my Bible.

Now, I'm not one to just open the Bible and read. I usually have a study I'm doing or a system. So, when I grabbed my Bible to read, I went to the scriptures of my current study. Well, that's what I meant to do, but what I actually did was turn to the wrong book by *mistake* so that the first thing my eyes went to was

written in red, words spoken by Jesus. It was Mark 11:22, which says, "Have faith in God," (KJV). That was it. That was all I read. And that was all I needed to read. That settled it for me.

You may ask, "Did things get easier?" Not really, but I knew that God was in this with me and that I would finish what I started. God had (has) a plan for my life, and I had to trust that this was part of it. If he brought me to it, he would bring me through it! Not long after that, I remember a particular clinical day that was difficult, and I was ready to quit again. At lunch, I went to a park at the river in Little Washington. I was sitting in my car listening to a tape by Karen Wheaton and praying.

This song came on entitled "Unworthy of the Blood." The words said, "A droplet of his precious blood then falls upon my name." At that very moment, I had this vision of me kneeling at the foot of the cross, and I was so ugly from sin, I was so unworthy that I couldn't even look up at Jesus and his sacrifice on the cross. Just as the song said those words, in the vision, I saw a drop of his precious blood actually fall on my head, and I was now worthy to look up at him. I immediately felt a power I had never before felt. The Holy Spirit engulfed me right there in my car. It was a presence I could almost touch. From that moment on, I had a whole new perspective of God's love for me, of his blood sacrifice and the power it contains.

God put so many wonderful people in my pathway, and I was blessed to call them friends, as well as spiritual advisors. Not long after I had the vision, three of my friends from church invited me to a revival ser-

TERRY L. SELLERS

vice. I went, although I can't tell you who the speaker was or anything from his sermon. What I can tell you is what happened after his sermon. He came over to me and took me by the hands. He had me step out and face him and then for several minutes he just stood there and cried *like a baby*!

Finally, he looked at me and said, "God showed me that there is a lot of hurt in your past. God said that people have misunderstood you all of your life." He continued to weep as he told me how God wanted to heal all of my hurt. I didn't know this man from Adam, but I knew the people I was with, and I knew they didn't tell him anything about me because they didn't know my past either. I was the only person there who knew my story. That's how I knew this man was genuine and that God had to have shown him the things he spoke. So, you can imagine how his words penetrated my heart. You might also imagine how much more my faith in God grew that night as God told me through this man that he knew me and he cared about me.

In my quiet times with God, I often listened to music. Around this same time, there was a song on a Ron Kenoly CD with lyrics that said, "If you can use anything, God, you can use me." After the day at the river and the night at this church, that song had truly become my prayer. God was showing me that, regardless of my past sin or hurt, he could use it all if I would give it to him. One day, while singing that same song, God revealed a glimpse of my past to me.

God took me back to that scariest, loneliest night of my life, and he reminded me of that little girl. You know, the little girl in the bed beside me who woke

up; hugged me; said, "I love you"; and then rolled back over fast asleep. God showed me that those were the only arms he had to hug me with at that moment in my life when I most needed him. And that mouth was the only mouth he had at that moment to tell me he loved me, when I needed to hear it the most. Wow!

How does it all fit? Even though I felt unworthy (and I was unworthy), his blood cleansed me. And even though I had a lot of hurt in me, he wanted to heal me. Even when I felt I couldn't make it, that I was going to fail again, if I kept my faith in him according to Mark 11:22, I would not fail. Not only that, God would use me if I would allow him to. He wanted me to be his hands, his feet, and his mouth. In fact, that's why I'm sharing my story with you now. Before God could use me, he had to change me. He couldn't change me until I wanted to be changed, and he couldn't use what I wouldn't give him, hurts and all. Yes, God can use anything. He once used a donkey to speak, but I wanted to be obedient so God wouldn't have to use a donkey in my stead.

Maybe you're at a place that I was. Maybe you think God has left you all alone, wondering how a so-called loving God says he cares for you when all you know is heartache and pain. Maybe the hurts of yesterday suppress any hopes of tomorrow and it seems that no one knows or cares, especially not God. I can tell you with all certainty that he does! Let's go back to Matthew 6: 25–34 and read again as God speaks to us from the Sermon on the Mount. I only quoted part of the scriptures before, but read for yourself how

TERRY L. SELLERS

God cares about the birds and the lilies and how much more valuable you are than that.

I know what it's like to hurt. There's a part of me that wants to hug every prostitute, drug addict, abused child, battered wife, so-called *lowlife,* and prisoner, telling him or her of God's great love. The world is full of hurting people who desperately need to know someone cares. They need to hear the words "I love you" and know that it's real. And those people aren't just in the ghettos of New York or living in a third-world country. I'm also talking about those in corporate offices wearing Armani suits with huge bank accounts while, underneath it all, they are filled with loneliness and hurt. God's provision isn't just about your checkbook balance. It's much deeper than that, so much deeper.

If we'll only listen, God wants so much to speak to each of us. He does it in the simple, yet profound ways such as this. One day, I was leaving my granddaddy's house after a visit. I had my nieces and youngest brother with me when Courtney looked at me and said, "Aunt Terry, can I sing you a song?" Now, one never knew what Courtney would say or do. In fact, in church one night, she had the entire congregation almost rolling in the floor when she refused to sit down because she wanted to sing. (Maybe she got that from me.) The preacher told my sister to just let her sing, and so she did—*Five Little Monkeys Jumping on the Bed!* I wasn't there that night, but I laughed until it hurt as my sister called and shared this story with me.

So, there we were in my car, and Courtney wanted to sing—to me! I just smiled and said *sure;* how could

I not? This is what she sang: "Jesus Loves Aunt Terry!" Nothing more, nothing less. She then looked at me and asked, "Do you like it?" Are you kidding? How precious was that and how like my God! I may have been unworthy of the blood, but God loved me just the same, and he used not only his Word to tell me but also the mouth of babes and even strangers. But just so you know, we're none worthy and we're none so good that we don't need God or his Son's blood covering. Whatever stain you have, let the blood drop on it. I assure you, there will be healing and forgiveness. And, yes, Courtney, I loved your song then and now.

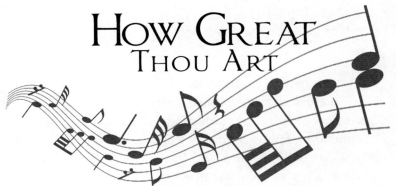

HOW GREAT THOU ART

Oh Lord my God! When I in awesome wonder
Consider all the worlds Thy Hands have made;
I see the stars, I hear the rolling thunder
Thy pow'r throughout the universe displayed:
Refrain:
Then sings my soul, my Savior God, to Thee,
HOW GREAT THOU ART!
  HOW GREAT THOU ART!
Then sings my soul, my Savior God, to Thee,
HOW GREAT THOU ART!
  HOW GREAT THOU ART!
When through the woods and forest glades I wander
And hear the birds sing sweetly in the trees;
When I look down from lofty mountain grandeur
And see the brook, and feel the gentle breeze:
And when I think that God, His Son not sparing,
Sent Him to die - I scarce can take it in,
That on the Cross, my burden gladly bearing,
He bled and died to take away my sin:
When Christ shall come with shout of acclamation
And take me home - what joy shall fill my heart!
Then I shall bow in humble adoration,
And then proclaim, my God
  HOW GREAT THOU ART!

—Stuart K. Hine.

Bless the Lord, O my soul, and all that is within me, bless his holy name.

Psalm 103:1

As you might have suspected, I did finish college—with honors at that. I don't say that boastfully, just giving God the praise from someone who started out feeling like a failure, someone who was often told that she didn't use her mind, and from someone who was once told she would *never* make it. So, here I was, still a new Christian, even though I had been raised in the church. Now I was a college graduate. I had no experience, but I did have a ten-thousand-dollar debt due to college loans. What a way to start!

In my church, I was now assisting with the youth group per request of the youth pastor. I really felt like I was in a place spiritually that God was using me and where he wanted me to be. I was also getting solid, practical teaching and learning about the Bible. God was allowing me to grow spiritually and to also help grow others, to give a part of myself to try and change other lives eternally. I certainly wasn't perfect, then or now, but I was being transformed with each step. Abraham Lincoln said it this way: "I do the very best I know how…and I mean to keep on doing it to the end."

But there was a problem. Now I had to find a job, and I couldn't. I was starting to panic because I had bills to pay, and I no longer had an income. Before I was living on my GI Bill and college loans, but that ended with graduation. I prayed and prayed, and it seemed that everything—and I do mean *everything*, whether I was reading from the Bible or from a devotional, lis-

TERRY L. SELLERS

tening to a sermon or a song, no matter what—seemed to say the same thing: "Wait on the Lord!"

I knew God must be trying to tell me something. You couldn't fool me. I mean, the Bible must say, "Wait on the Lord," in a thousand different places, and I'm sure I came across them all. No, you couldn't fool me. I got it! Actually, "Wait on the Lord" is mentioned in only forty-two scriptures in that reference, but I must have read or heard every single verse at least fifty times each—no joke. (Maybe my mom was right; maybe my head was hard.) I would learn though that God's time and my time were two different things. Jentezen Franklin makes the point clear when he made this statement in a recent sermon: "God lives in eternity, and he doesn't wear a wristwatch!"

In the meantime, I was applying for jobs, but I could find none locally in my profession. I didn't feel like God wanted me to move or to return home, so I began to apply for jobs outside of my field. I even applied to be a bank teller and to be a dishwasher. Not that there's anything wrong with either of those jobs. God bless the people who do them, but I was certain neither was for me, especially washing dishes. I'm not big on anything that has to do with the kitchen. Incidentally, I didn't get those jobs. The person I interviewed with for both told me they didn't want to spend time and money to train me because they knew that when a job became available in my field I would leave them. It made sense to me, but it didn't solve my problem.

Eventually, a couple in the church that had become so dear and like my own family hired me part-time to help in their painting business. The church also hired me to paint the entire education wing. This was also not a job I desired but one that God provided and one for which I was thankful. The two jobs together didn't amount to enough income to pay my bills, and I soon found myself in a financial dilemma.

The electric company sent me a notice saying that my lights were going to be cut off if my bill wasn't paid within a matter of days. Really, that didn't matter because I was about to be evicted anyway. I had little food, and I had no money to cover the bills. In fact, one creditor who called me inquired, "If things are that bad, then just how are you living?" To that, I replied, "By the grace of God." Smugly, she said, "That's funny, but really, how are you living?" With all certainty I responded, "Really, by the grace of God!" It was all I could do to afford gas to go paint and to get to church. Even in all of that, I remained faithful in my tithe and offering as the Bible commanded me.

Few people knew of my circumstances, which probably had more to do with my pride than anything. However, one friend who did know went to the church on my behalf. I was then contacted by the pastor and asked to come in and talk with him. After having heard my circumstances, he gave me a solution. The pastor said that I should move out of my apartment, letting my security deposit cover my rent that was due. He said that my friend who had went to him on my behalf had agreed to let me live with her for a while, and he stated that he knew a couple in the church who would be willing to store my belongings. The church would pay my light bill, and I could keep painting for income until I got a job and got back on my feet.

TERRY L. SELLERS

After he finished, I just didn't feel peace so I respectfully asked my pastor if I could go home and pray about things. I told him that I would return at 4:00 p.m. that day with my decision. I did just that, and when I returned that afternoon, I had my answer from God. While praying, God reminded me of the things he had been teaching me in the scriptures. He also gave me such peace, a confident assurance deep within about my response to my pastor. I explained to him (as if I needed to) that the Bible does not say that I would lose everything I had but it does say that my God would supply my every need. So, although I appreciated all that was offered, I was going to *wait on the Lord* as he had been telling me in his Word. Again, few knew of my situation, but this is how the next few days unfolded.

I came home from painting one day to find groceries at my door. To this day, I don't know who left them there. That night, a man in the church called me and said that he may have misheard what he was going to say but that he felt like God was telling him to pay my rent for the month. And so he did. The church did pay my light bill, and someone else in the church called and asked me if I could meet her at the gas station. She said she felt like God told her to fill up my gas tank. That was a good thing because the next day I got a call from a hospital about thirty-five to forty miles away offering me an immediate job in my profession starting the next day, without an interview but based solely on a personal reference!

How could I deny that God was real or that he cared about me? It was a very difficult and a very humbling time, accepting these gifts, God's provision, and especially learning to wait on the Lord. I often wondered what would have happened had I just followed the advice given me without seeking God's will for myself or without standing in faith, believing God would provide.

If there was ever a song that was my absolute favorite, it would have to be "How Great Thou Art." That song began to come alive deep within me during this time. By now, God had shown himself to be so faithful, so great, over and over again to me. I could not even sing this song without choking up or crying. It was hard to grasp the love of my Savior when I had felt so unlovable for the better part of my life. In fact, the first part of this book's title is actually taken from this song: "Then sings my soul" became *Songs of My Soul.* God has taken a life of brokenness and has given me reasons to sing.

I don't understand how a person can look at creation and not believe in God. He is so great! There's not a star in the sky he didn't put there, and no star will fall to earth without his knowledge of it. The earth is full of God's power and majesty, in every sunrise and with every wave that crashes onto the shore. There's so much beauty in his creation, yet he still cares about me and the smallest details of my life. He cares about you and the smallest details of your life.

Take a caterpillar, for instance. It goes through this metamorphosis—a change from the inside out—and it becomes this thing of beauty: a butterfly, with wings to fly. I was at a point in my life where God was beginning a metamorphosis in me, deep from within. The Bible says in Isaiah 61:3 that God will give you beauty

TERRY L. SELLERS

for ashes. My life had been a heap of ashes. Until now, God had been leveling the ground under my feet and making it solid again, or maybe for the first time. But now, God was going deeper to deal with the junk in my life, the hidden places, to heal the scars.

During this time, one of the toughest things I came to realize was that I had anger and bitterness toward my parents. It didn't belong in my heart, so I starting praying about it. My answer was to write them letters.

The letter to my dad was, surprisingly, the easiest to write. I told him that I forgave him, and I asked for forgiveness for the anger I harbored against him. I also told him that I cared about him and that I hated to see him destroying his life with alcohol. I begged him to stop drinking. I spoke about God and his soul and told him that if I could give him anything in this world, I would give him salvation, but that was a decision he had to make on his own, one I prayed he would make.

The letter to my mom was harder to write. I realized that I had so much resentment and bitterness toward her. It was awful to see this truth in my heart. The only way I knew to be free of it was to do as the Bible said: confess my sins and ask for her forgiveness. I knew that the letter would hurt her, but I also knew it was something I had to do. I couldn't say the things in my heart in person because communication was not a strong part of our relationship—in my family at all, to be exact. I really prayed before I wrote the letter, and it was emotionally draining for me. I had recently heard someone say, "Don't ever make your failures

your dwelling place," and I was determined to move past my failures.

On the day I knew the letter would arrive, I had three of my close friends at my house. When my phone rang and I confirmed it was my mom, they began to pray. I sat on my bathroom floor and cried at the pain I had so obviously caused her as I listened to her response. But when it was over, things were different. From that day on, God began to change the relationship between me and my mom. He also began to change my heart, and he gave me a love for her that I never had before. I'm sure God did the same thing in her. Also, about eight months later, my dad told me that he hadn't touched alcohol in almost *eight months*! That wasn't just coincidence. God was repairing my home.

The next couple of years were mostly good. I continued to grow in my faith, mostly through trials on my job. Hey, new territory, new trials, and boy, did I have trials! A situation in particular comes to mind. One morning a co-worker made a serious false accusation against me, stating that I assaulted her. Now, back in the day, one thing I did have if nothing else was a quick temper fueled by years of anger, and I would react first, think later. This girl worked hard to stir my anger, but I can assure you I never assaulted her or even came close.

On this particular day, it was 7:00 a.m. and change of shifts. I was her relief, so there was no one present for my defense. After the perceived occurrence (our hands touched while reaching for the telephone), she called the hospital police, who promptly came and took a report from us both, at the end of which he con-

cluded that there was no assault. I knew that I hadn't assaulted her, but because she made the accusation and because the hospital had a zero-tolerance policy, I was suspended from my job for two weeks.

If you think I just swallowed that in faith, think again. I had a very difficult time, and a part of me wanted so much to retaliate. I struggled with anger and even hate toward that person and for quite some time. Eventually, God helped me find peace and forgiveness. That's not to say that I wasn't to blame either. I knew her personality, and I should have just walked away. Many things come to mind where I wish I could have a *do-over*. Job relationships and situations probably top the list. Regardless, I was learning with each new step and mostly from taking the wrong step.

But God was faithful to direct me back on track. Before long, I was out of debt, and I was able to purchase my first home. I was truly a blessed person. I had so many great friends, a wonderful church family, a good job with co-workers that were also like family (despite the situation above), and I had a family that I loved very much. It was also a growing family as this funny little guy came into our lives, my nephew, Chandler. Oh God, how great thou art!

THROUGH IT ALL

I've had many tears and sorrows;
I've had questions for tomorrow;
There've been times I didn't know right from wrong;
But in every situation, God gave blessed consolation,
That my trials come to only make me strong.
Chorus:
THROUGH IT ALL,
THROUGH IT ALL,
Oh I've learned to trust in Jesus,
I've learned to trust in God.
THROUGH IT ALL,
THROUGH IT ALL,
Oh I've learned to depend upon His Word.
I've been to lots of places,
And I've seen a lot of faces;
There've been times I felt so all alone;
But in my lonely hours, yes,
    those precious lonely hours,
Jesus lets me know that I was His own.
I thank God for the Mountains,
And I thank Him for the valleys;
I thank Him for the storms He brought me through;
For if I'd never had a problem,
I wouldn't know that He could solve them,
I'd never know what faith in God could do.

—Andraé Crouch

> The Lord will send His faithful love by day; His song will be with me in the night—a prayer to the God of my life.
>
> Psalm 42:8 (HCSB)

I don't know if one would ever consider me a role model but if ever I had a little protégé, it would have to be my niece, Ashley. Maybe it's because she and I spent more time together than my other nieces and I. That's not because I loved them any less, but only due to life's circumstances when Ashley was younger.

Anyway, one day Ashley and I were preparing to go somewhere when I noticed that her shirt was dirty around the bottom edges. I tried to no avail to get Ashley to change into a clean shirt; she just wouldn't do so. Finally, I asked her to just tuck her shirt inside her jeans to hide the spot. Well, she didn't want to do that either.

I was trying not to get frustrated, but for the life of me, I could not understand what the big deal was. Finally, Ashley told me that my shirt wasn't tucked in. I responded by showing her that it was because I had a hole by one of my belt loops and I was trying to hide it. Do you know what she did? She pulled up her shirt and looked and looked on her jeans to find something that resembled a hole and then showed it to me.

That's when it hit me. She didn't want to change her clothes because she was dressed just like me. In fact, my sister was the one who first clued me in to the fact that both of her daughters copied my life so much. When the light finally came on in my head on this particular day, I just said okay to Ashley. But inside,

TERRY L. SELLERS

my heart swelled. I mean, isn't imitation the highest form of compliment?

Why am I sharing this story with you? It's because being a Christian doesn't mean that one is now better than another. What it means, or should mean, is that a person now desires to imitate the life of Christ. It is a daily journey, and sometimes more of a minute-by-minute trek.

I knew that inside of me I truly wanted to be a different person. I knew my heart, and it wasn't pretty, far from being Christ-like in too many ways. But the desire was there. God would answer that desire because it is his desire for us to be more like him and to have a more personal relationship with him. Someone once told me that after you ask Christ into your life, you have him, and you can't have more or less of him. I disagree. When we ask God into our hearts, he says in his Word that he won't leave us (although we have the choice to leave him). But *we can* know him more intimately, just as with any relationship. I wanted more!

Can I tell you that nothing in life will cause you to seek God more, to develop your relationship with him more, than trials? And do you know that some of the hardest trials you will *ever* go through will be within the church walls? I don't proclaim to be some super Christian with this vast knowledge and wisdom to share with you. I'm just me. What goodness I might have is because of Christ in me, and most of my knowledge is from life's experiences and the Word alone. Unfortunately, some of that experience did come from problems within the church.

The details of the trials I faced in the church aren't

really important. I don't need to rehash them. The important thing is what I learned from them. I guess the greatest tragedy would be to go through such trials and to not learn anything. Perhaps greater yet would be to come out on the other side and to harbor wrong feelings, such as anger, or to lose relationships or to just give up and walk away from God and the church. I've seen it happen too many times.

The people that are the hardest to reach are those who have been offended by someone in the church or by someone who claimed to be a Christian. I certainly didn't want that to be the outcome of my situation. If you're one of those people, someone who has walked away from God because of someone in the church or because of another Christian, please allow me to say I'm sorry on behalf of the person who hurt you. I beg you not to let this keep you out of heaven. Just because a person is in the church, it does not mean they are a Christian or infallible. Joyce Meyer often says that she can stay in her garage all day, but it won't make her a car.

I was really hurt by fellow believers. It's okay to say that because what the world needs is for us to just be real. The fact is, people are people whether they are in the church or not, and people hurt each other. I'm sure I have hurt others in and out of the church. It hasn't been my intention to do so, but I'm just as human as the ones who have hurt me. And if I told you that I handled everything in a perfect manner or that I did nothing wrong, I would not be honest. I simply did the best I could at the time.

I did learn a valuable lesson through all of the hurt. I learned that I needed to keep my faith in God alone,

TERRY L. SELLERS

not in my pastor, my Sunday school teacher, my spiritual mentor, or even in my closest Christian friends. Sometimes it's easy to trust in these people more than we should. We may even place them on a pedestal, thinking they're more holy than the rest of us because of their position or their title. But that's not fair to them, nor is it true. We're all human, and we all sin and fall short of the glory of God. Isn't that what the Bible says in Romans 3:23?

I just love the words to the song "Through It All." Life is about the journey and the trials we face along the way. I am thankful for the trials because they keep me pointed to God and they grow my strength. I'm even thankful for the very painful hurts that came from fellow believers because, more than anything, it allowed me to see my misplaced faith and trust and to give that back to God. We have to ultimately depend upon him and his Word alone. God has a way of getting us to realize that truth, if we just seek it. When speaking about the trials of life, Jentezen Franklin said, "God is more interested in developing your character than in solving your problems." I needed more character development!

During this same time in my life, I began to feel like God wanted to change something. It was just a feeling that wouldn't go away, and one day it dawned on me what that change was; I needed to move. I don't know why. Maybe I was too comfortable where I was. I had a nice home. I was blessed with great friends. My co-workers were like family now, and I had a good job and church, despite the trials. Life was comfortable.

I didn't want to move. I think I was truly happy for the first time in my life. But the feeling persisted, so I began to pray about it. As I did, things began to happen to confirm what God was speaking to me. Out of the blue, I got a phone call from a job recruiter. How he got my name and home phone number is beyond me, but he called to tell me about available jobs that just so happened to be in the same area I felt God was directing me to. Maybe that was just coincidence.

On another day, I was on the way to the mall with a good friend of mine when she started questioning me in direct relation to me moving, and she named the exact city. I hadn't said a word to anyone at all about moving, much less a location. *Strange,* I thought. And that was the end of that conversation. She never said why she asked me that. I never inquired why she was asking, and we've never mentioned it since. The thing that really got to me though was the numerous days I would return home to find fliers or notes on my front door from people or realtors desiring to buy my home. *My home was not for sale!* There was no sign in my front yard. I even looked around to see if other homes had the same fliers. If they did, I didn't see them, so why mine?

One day, my aforementioned friend and her family were at my home. We were going to dinner, and they had come to pick me up. Just as we were about to leave, we saw our pastor and his family walking around the neighborhood looking at a few places that actually *were* for sale. By this time, I had accepted the fact that God wanted me to move, and I had told my friend. I didn't yet know the specifics such as when. That didn't

TERRY L. SELLERS

matter to her; she took the liberty (in faith) to mention that my home would soon be for sale, and they asked to look at it. I actually got an offer then and there for my entire home, contents and all. Although I didn't take the offer then, their son did buy my house months later.

I wish I had written down all of the ways God confirmed things to me. I believe that is how God works. He whispers his desire for us in our ears, in our hearts. We just have to listen. Once we know what he is saying, God then begins to confirm it in ways that only he can. It's up to us to listen and to obey.

Eventually, I decided to share with my boss what I thought God was telling me and that I would be moving in the near future. Word was starting to get around that I was looking for another job. I didn't want to hide things; I wanted to be open and honest. I also began to share these things with a friend, my co-worker. Weeks after I had told her all the things that led up to my decision and after her seeing things fall into place, she said to me, "I may not be a Christian (in practice) but even I can see that this is what God wants for you."

Before long, God worked out all of the details, and I was on my way to the Raleigh-Durham area. I guess where faith was concerned, God was teaching me in steps. This was the biggest step yet. I had no connections to this area. I just knew that I wanted my life to imitate the life of Christ, like Ashley wanted to imitate mine, and I knew that I wanted to be obedient. I really felt like God was calling me to move to this area to support a new church plant, an extension of my church from Greenville, and to be a part of a planned

children's ministry that the new church plant was to one day start. Other than that, I had no direction but to go. And so I did, depending on God's Word *through it all*, knowing that he had already brought me through many storms, as the song says!

THAT'S NO MOUNTAIN

I looked at that mountain that stood in my way,
Would this be my last climb, could this be my fate?
How my heart beat so fearful, what challenge awaits,
But, strength rose up in me, God's power and grace.
Chorus:
That's no mountain for a climber,
    I know what awaits at the peak
Jesus is there watching over, to see if His
    help I should need.
He makes sure that His dear precious children
Don't fall by the trial so steep.
That's no mountain for a climber,
When the maker of the mountain is standing by me.
I beheld all the footprints that had been there before,
Up through the cliffs and the rocks,
Till I could see them no more.
And, I wondered what brave ones
Would challenge such feat,
God said "it's the saints, child, that's gone
    on before thee."

—Gerald Crabb

Come, let us sing for joy to the LORD; let us shout
aloud to the Rock of our salvation.

Psalm 95:1

That move was over six years ago. I wish I could tell
you that life has been bliss since then. The truth is that
it has been anything but bliss. I could write a novel on
the last six years alone. It would be pretty depressing
in parts, although God has taught me to look at all the
good things during those same six years. More than
anything, he has taught me to just sing! There is power
in praise, and music does wonders to lift the spirit.

No, I'm not going to write out those years, but I
am going to tell you about some of my life events during this time. The song I've chosen for this chapter
of my life I actually owe to a dear friend of mine. I've
purposely not mentioned many names in this book
because I don't wish to offend anyone or to leave anyone out, but this name I need to mention. Her name
was Lisa, and I'll never forget the day that I was at her
home and she shared this song with me. The title was
"That's No Mountain," and the very next words say
"for a climber."

I met Lisa in X-ray school in 1992. We became fast
and close friends. I guess it was five years later that she
was diagnosed with breast cancer. Even though I was
in the diagnostic medical field, at the time, this was the
closest that cancer had come to touch my life personally.
I watched Lisa in her battle, and I delighted when she
returned to her faith in God through this battle.

We actually became closer during this time in her
life. She touched me not only with her faith that grew

each day, but also with her fight for survival. She told me once that every single day she lived was worth any pain because she wanted to be there for her son and husband as long as she could. How unselfish! What sacrifice! I prayed for Lisa, and I expected a miracle, but there came a point when we both knew it was terminal. It was during this time, while visiting with her, Lisa had me sit in her car out in the garage as she played this song for me. Afterwards, she spoke candidly with me about her battle, her renewed faith, and why this song had come to mean so much. You might say it went from being Lisa's song to being my own. I've been climbing ever since.

I moved from Greenville in August of 2002. Just one month later, my heart broke as Lisa went on to heaven. Perhaps that is why she has a chapter in my book, because she's not here to write her own story. Regardless, I was happy for her because she was now healed and in heaven. *She finished her climb.* But I was also sad, as it was a difficult loss for me. I truly believed for a miracle. So, where did that leave me in my faith when she died? Actually, it's pretty simple. I still took God at his Word; I still believed, then and now.

Like I've alluded to before, I'm not a philosopher, and I'm no Bible scholar. To me, you either accept faith or you don't. It is not a *seeing is believing* thing. I did question God, but what God did was remind me of my own words to Lisa during the early days of her sickness. I had told her that I was praying for a miracle, for her healing. But sometimes God chooses to heal on this side of heaven; sometimes he chooses to

heal on the other side of heaven. I just wanted to know that she would be in heaven.

Do you know or recall the Bible story in chapter three of Daniel about the three Hebrew men who were thrown into the fiery furnace because they wouldn't bow down to King Nebuchadnezzar's idols? To paraphrase what they said in verses 17–18, "I know God is well able to deliver us, *but if he does not . . . !*" (emphasis added) That's it. That's faith.

Faith does not mean that you ask God for something, believe it will happen, and *poof!*, there it is! Faith means that you trust God no matter the outcome. As for Lisa, she is healed, and she is in heaven. That's what really matters in the end. God gave me something precious to hold on to—that truth and the memories of the friendship we shared—and my life is better for it.

I don't know what cross you carry, what burden you bear, what mountain you face. Maybe you've lost someone close to you. Maybe you've been abused or you were the abuser. Maybe you're sick or have cancer yourself. Maybe you carry the shame of abortion. You may have been unfaithful in your marriage, or your spouse was unfaithful to you. You may be struggling with a life-controlling addiction, or you may even be a murderer. The list of struggles is inexhaustible, but so is God's grace.

We all have things that define us and people that leave footprints in our hearts, for good or bad. I say that reluctantly because they only define us if we allow them to. But nothing is too great for God. No matter how high the mountain may loom or how great a shadow of despair it may cast in your life, if you just

TERRY L. SELLERS

press on in faith, God will help you climb, and there is a better life at the top or on the other side. I've climbed a few mountains in my time, and one thing I can say is that the view gets better the higher you go; just keep climbing. Maybe the outcome won't be what you hope for, what you expect, but you will still win when God is in it.

I can honestly say that this move was certainly not going as I had hoped. Aside from Lisa's death, the job I had taken was becoming a nightmare. I began looking and applying for other jobs in just two months. I was dreading going to work every day. In December, not even four months after my move, there was a big ice storm that paralyzed the entire area. I didn't have electricity for eight days, and I was trying to study for a national board exam that was just a few weeks away. It was to obtain another credential in my chosen field and the first exam of two that was all physics, not my best subject.

Since I was new to the area, I didn't know many people yet. Those I did know were also without electricity, so I just slept in my apartment with no heat for two nights. The temperatures dropped below forty degrees and, as a result, I got really sick. On the eighth night without power, I was so tired and so sick that I went to stay in a hotel. (At last, I could find a room available now that most of the emergency electric workers were leaving town.) The next morning, as I drove to work, I remember praying and asking God when my last day at this job would be. Little did I know, it would be that very day, as I was terminated.

Let me just say that I had never been fired before and, although their reason for the termination was *because they knew I was unhappy and looking for another job,* I was still so humiliated. Here I was, new to the area; I didn't know anyone well. I had no electricity in this winter wonderland, and I was sick. I had a major exam in two weeks, and it was also December, which meant Christmas. Now I was fired—no income! I was devastated. Was this what stepping out in faith was all about?

That evening, while there was still daylight left, I went back to my apartment to pack some things and to decide what my next move would be. While I was there, my cell phone rang, and it was my friend from back in Greenville, the same one who told me that even she could see that this move was what God wanted me to do. What irony! As we talked and she kept asking what was wrong, I finally admitted to her the events of my day.

She was so sweet. She told me that I could come back *home* and that I could stay with her family until I found another place to live. She said she was certain that I could get my job back because our employer had told me before I left that they would find a place for me if I ever wanted to return. She was working out all the details, but as I listened, my faith rose up in me. I told her that I really appreciated all she offered but I couldn't do that. God didn't bring me here for me to just run back home at the first sign of trouble. In fact, this was my home now.

She asked me what I was going to do, and then it became clear. I told her that first, I was going to use the time off to study, take the exam, and pass it. Next,

TERRY L. SELLERS

I would enjoy the two weeks' paid vacation (severance) I was given at Christmas by spending time with my family and friends. Then, I would get a job. Can I just tell you what happened? First, I took the exam, and I passed it. Next, I went to Greenville to celebrate the Christmas holiday with my friends a little early, and then I went back home to be with my family.

While my sister and I were shopping at Myrtle Beach, my cell phone rang. It was the administrator of a company calling to offer me a job. He told me that if I just accepted his offer and came to work on December 30, I would then be off until January 2, but I would start that year with full benefits, including their contributions to my 401K. And so I did!

I enjoyed the holiday with my family. I went to my new job, and I never missed the first paycheck. I was never without insurance or health benefits, and I've worked there ever since. God was faithful once again. What the liar meant for evil, God used for good. In his faithfulness, God will continue to stretch us and to grow us. This was only my first four months since I had stepped out in what I felt he called me to do. I had much more stretching and growing to come, many more mountains to climb, but I was and still am a climber.

UNFAILING LOVE

You have my heart
And I am Yours forever
You are my strength
God of grace and power
And everything
You hold in your hand
Still you make time for me
I can't understand
Praise you God of earth and sky
How beautiful is Your unfailing love
Unfailing love
You never change, God, You remain
The Holy One and my unfailing love
Unfailing love
You are my rock
The One I hold on to
You are my song
And I sing for you.

—Ed Cash, Cary Pierce, and Chris Tomlin.

I will sing of the LORD's great love forever; with my mouth I will make your faithfulness known through all generations.

—Psalm 89:1

Like I said in the last chapter, the move was not easy. I stepped out in faith to do something I felt God was leading me to do. Although it has been over six years now, nothing was like I expected. I really didn't have a long list of expectations, but in my mind, I thought, *If God wants this, it must be good, right?* Well, not so far. Each year was harder than the prior one. Even in all of that, I still believe the move was the thing God wanted. There's always good in the journey, if we just look.

Believe me when I tell you that my life has been one test or trial right after the other. Difficult doesn't even begin to describe it. Even so, I wouldn't change it because I know God says he has a purpose for all things and that he will use my trials to change me for the better. In fact, somewhere along the way, I came across an article written by David Wilkerson in which he said that not every trial was a test but sometimes it's training. What God was training me for, I didn't know, but I did trust him.

The thing about this time in my life is that I can't really share the details with you for different reasons. On my job, I have gone through some very difficult things. Since I still work at this job, I can't share the details, but it mostly has to do with one person. As for my family, I know I haven't mentioned them much, but I can say that I've watched things go from bad to worse year after year. I jokingly refer to things as

TERRY L. SELLERS

the Sellers Saga because it just never seems to end or to get any better. Like I said before, there is always drama where my family is concerned. But it's no joke; it breaks my heart.

I will share a general overview. At one point, my mom was recovering from a near call with death. She spent eight days on life support, and the doctors said it was a miracle that she didn't die or that she didn't lose her leg. When she came home, she could no longer do the simple daily tasks like bathing, cooking, etc. Although she did get some better with time, she was never the same, and she was now much weaker and needed help. My dad, who had been in prison, was sent home pretty much to die, as he was terminally ill. I had one sibling whose marriage was in turmoil and falling apart at the time, and the situations surrounding it were stressful to say the very least. One sibling was in prison, another was struggling with an addiction, and the other one was constantly getting in trouble with the law.

My mom, who could barely care for herself, was left to care for two small grandchildren due to the situations; one was an infant, my newest niece, Brittany. That in and of itself is another sad, hurtful story, as we would later learn that she wasn't truly my brother's child. The betrayal and lies not only hurt my brother but it hurt us all as she was eventually taken from us. We loved her so much. In our hearts, she always will be family.

Another of my nieces moved in with my mom due to situations in her home. She helped Mama out with the younger ones during the week, although she was

a senior in high school. On the weekends, she had to work, so I would travel five hours round-trip to help with the children, keep up my mom's yard and home, help both her and my dad out, and do my dad's shopping. This was all because the struggles of my siblings took over their lives, and they weren't there to help for the most part. This went on for almost five months with me traveling every weekend. It was exhausting both physically and emotionally as I also had my own home, responsibilities, and trials to deal with the other five days of the week.

The list of struggles goes on, but to share them would be to share details of their lives, and I don't feel that is my place. Suffice it to say that there has been a lot of pain for us all. Even though it was their lives, it caused me a lot of heartache because I love them and it hurt me to see them hurt, especially when I knew life didn't have to be that way. Some of their decisions affected me directly, in ways they probably never stopped to consider. Some of their responsibilities became my life for a while, but I was thankful to be able to help as I could.

Aside from that, what my family and most everyone else in my life didn't know about was a very private, personal struggle I was going through. Again, I can't share the details due to others and their privacy. To be honest, I still don't understand what happened or why I was even being tested in such a way. It was a battle that caused me to examine my faith in ways I've never known.

I began to question God. I also began to slip into a depression that would only grow over time, and

TERRY L. SELLERS

because of the sensitive nature of things, I felt I had no one to turn to. I felt like the double-minded man that Paul speaks about in James 1:8, unstable in all my ways. All of my life, I had believed in God, even if I hadn't served him, but now the very core of that belief was being challenged. There was no area of my life left unscathed. I had troubles with my family, on my job, with my health, in my finances, with my emotions, in my church, and now with my very faith in God.

There was a long period of time when I couldn't even pray. Reading my Bible was only a thought of what I should do. It seemed like my close relationships were drifting apart and like I was in this deep pit with no way out. All I could say to God was, "I don't know." It didn't even make sense. It was like one day I woke up and I just didn't know my purpose anymore. I didn't know why I took the steps that lead to this place, and I surely didn't know how to move on, where to go, what to do. The answers wouldn't come. God had them, but he allowed me to live in these questions.

One thing I did do in all of this was I continued to listen to Christian music. It was a solace, and the songs seemed to bring me strength. My car radio dial stayed tuned to KLOVE, a Christian station. One song that was popular at this time was, "Unfailing Love," sung by Chris Tomlin and Steven Curtis Chapman. One verse of that song in particular seemed to be my life-line. It said, "You are my Rock, the One I hold on to." Even though I felt like I was on sinking sand, I wasn't. I stood on the Rock, and I was holding on with everything I had. You see, in Psalms, the Bible uses *Rock* as a reference to God. That's not just a pebble

(although that's all David needed to defeat Goliath), but it's a boulder, immoveable by human hands. That was my solace. God was my Rock, and he wasn't going anywhere.

Maybe I can't share the details from this particular time in my life with you—sometimes our struggles are that deep and that personal—but I can share with you what I walked away from that trial with: the knowledge I gained. And maybe, just maybe, that will save you some steps of heartache, or maybe you will find encouragement for some trial you are in. After all, that's my whole purpose, my desire in writing all of this.

The first thing I learned is that I can't trust in my circumstances, only in the God of my circumstances. I heard Joyce Meyer say that trust requires us to have unanswered questions and we should get comfortable not knowing. Remember when I said that all I could say to God was "I don't know?" I had no clue why God had brought me to this place in my life, a place where I thought I was going to be used by him and for him yet all I had was one struggle after the next. I couldn't understand why there was still so much pain in my family. I really didn't understand the struggle with my job or more so with one co-worker in particular. Why did this person seem intent on marring my character? What had I done to them? And now here I was in this very deep, personal situation. Why?

During this time, I read Joyce Meyer's *Starting Your Day Right*, which said: "Be willing to obey God even when you don't understand what He is doing with you." (New York: Warner Books, Inc., 2003, 183). This summed up what I was learning as a whole. Another

TERRY L. SELLERS

thing I was learning was to just keep my mouth shut and to allow God to be my defense; this was particularly true with my job situation. I must admit, this area is still a struggle. When we've been mistreated, we naturally want to defend ourselves, but it takes more character not to. I believe the truth will eventually come to light. Even if it doesn't, God can use our silence to speak to others in ways words never could.

Where my family was concerned, I so wanted to rush in and save the day. I just knew the solution to all of their problems, and I wanted to tell them . But I couldn't. I had to learn to pray and to trust that God would do the work in his time. Sometimes, it takes people hitting rock bottom before they're willing to look up to see that God is there. It hurt to see my family hurting, but true love can require you to step aside so that God can step in. They may need to be there before they're willing to call on God. I can tell you that some of my family is still in that place, spiraling down, and it still hurts me, but I can't make decisions for them, only pray they make the right ones.

As I said before, one of the hardest things a Christian can go through is when they are hurt from within the church. I know this from experience, not once but twice now. Actually, it's more than one incident I speak of here, but in one case, I wasn't the recipient. I was affected indirectly as the situation unfolded, and I saw the struggles of people I really cared about. I still see the scars that were left in lives, not yet healed. The whole thing really grieved me. Once again, I say, no matter what title a person wears, be it pastor, deacon, teacher, pope, president, or church member, we're all

human, and we will all fail. And, sadly, we will hurt those around us. I think Gary Chapman said it best in *Love as a Way of Life* when he wrote, "To live is to have the potential of hurting others and being hurt." (Colorado Springs: Waterbrook Press, 2008, 70).

Again, I say, we shouldn't put anyone on a pedestal or think that they are any closer to God than us just because of their title or position. In reality, any one of us can have a close relationship with God if we desire it and if we take time for God. Part of this whole struggle in the church really made me take a good look at myself and at the church as a whole. I didn't really like what I saw. Sometimes, even though the Bible says to judge not, people in the church appoint themselves judge and jury.

Why is it that we in the church tend to judge the harshest? Isn't the church supposed to be a place where the sinner comes, just as he is, and finds love and acceptance? I began to realize that we *Christians*, me included, are so busy judging even our own within the church that we neglect to show the love and compassion of Christ, and we forget that our job is to help teach and disciple. We don't always accept people as they are and allow God to do the work that changes them. We sometimes have the expectation that if a person is on the inside of the church, they better be living *the life*. God alone is judge and I for one am thankful. He is compassionate, and his mercies are new every morning. I need that!

Out of my struggle with the church, I also learned that a person's title or position does not guarantee that they always seek God's will in a matter or that their

TERRY L. SELLERS

decisions or actions are without error. What happens when you feel that God's will for your life involves others to also be a part of that purpose, to be obedient to God, yet they give up and walk away or they don't even seem to realize it? The answer I came to was that God only holds me accountable for my actions in what he has asked of me. *Don't have faith in the outcome; have faith in God!*

During this time, I had someone close to me, my spiritual leader, make a statement directly to me that really hurt. Pretty much, what they said in not so many words was that they didn't trust what I felt God had spoken to me. I guess it hurt because I served in the church under them. If they didn't trust my life as a Christian and my ability to be led by the Spirit of God, how could they trust me to lead others? It took me awhile to let go of that hurt and to realize that my validation doesn't come from man but from God. How can someone else even know what God has said to you? Sometimes we give man more power than we should. When we get to heaven, we won't be held accountable for what others thought we did wrong; only for what God required.

As for my very personal, private struggle I was going through, I wish I could tell you that I understood it, but I didn't, not even now. I guess because of it, it was the ultimate thing that caused me to question God. And all of it together started me down a road of depression. I just didn't know what to think or feel anymore. I really didn't feel anything except loneliness and confusion. But that's just it. It doesn't matter what we feel. Feelings will lie to us. What matters is what we choose to

believe, and what I choose to believe was God, even in my depression and loneliness.

I know some will read this and judge me, saying that I shouldn't be depressed as a Christian. Well, I was. Many in the Bible fought depression, including King David. I think the world really needs Christians to just be real. Life is tough, period! Don't pretend that a life in Christ is worry-free. It isn't, and even the Bible tells us it won't be. The pastor said recently in his sermon that being a Christian is not for the faint of heart. He compared the Christian walk to a roller-coaster ride with highest highs and lowest lows and everything in between. I'm not saying that we need to go around complaining all the time by any means but, it's okay to just be human and to let others see our struggles. If not, how will they see our victories?

When I said a line from this chapter's soul song was my lifeline, I meant it. I had difficulty praying, and I didn't want to read my Bible. I had almost lost hope, yet I still stood in faith, expecting God to be everything he promised, even in my time of questioning him. I know it sounds crazy, but God was my *Rock, the one I held on to*, as the song says. The next line of the song says "you are my song and I sing to you." I like that. My knuckles were white; my fingernails were dug in deep. I was hanging on with all I had and even though I didn't feel like it, I kept singing! The only certainty I had of tomorrow was the one who held it. But that was all I needed because his love was and is unfailing!

TERRY L. SELLERS

CHAPTER FOURTEEN

Without music, life is a journey through desert.
—Pat Conray

I guess one of the saddest times in life is when the music stops and you have no song. That's what happened to me. Chapter three in the book of Ecclesiastes tells us that there is a time for everything, including a time to die. On October 18, 2006, my dad did just that. With his death, a part of me died. I had hopes and dreams; more specifically, I had prayed many prayers about things concerning my family that I now knew would not be, could not be answered. This was during the time of questioning my faith, so you can imagine how my faith took yet another blow.

On December 25, 2006, my dear, sweet Gram died. Even though Alzheimer's had stolen her from me some time before, this again was a hard thing. She was the backbone of our family and the truest example of Christ I had ever seen. Gram had a place in my heart that no one else could fill, and now there was a big gaping hole.

Then, on January 10, 2008, my mom went on to heaven. I can't begin to tell you how this turned my world upside down. I watched any hope I held onto slip away. My depression reached its lowest point, and loneliness set in like this life-sucking disease. It became my best friend again.

I couldn't understand it. I no longer wanted any part of my life as I knew it. I didn't want to work in my profession anymore. I didn't like where I worked. I didn't like where I lived, yet I had no desire to be anywhere else. I suddenly felt like I didn't belong in the church I was attending. I felt like a forty-year-old orphan. I had no desire, no dream, nothing. I don't know why I felt this way. Maybe it was because I no longer had either parent and it was an identity issue. All I know is that life as I knew it had now changed forever.

I can't give you any big life revelation because I didn't have one. All I know is how I felt and that, even though I had no song left, God held me through this time and he sang to me.

TERRY L. SELLERS

How Can I
Keep From Singing?

There is an endless song echoes in my soul
I hear the music ring
And though the storms may come
I am holding on
To the rock I cling
Chorus:
How can I keep from singing your praise
How can I ever say enough
How amazing is Your love
How can I keep from shouting Your name
I know I am loved by the King
And it makes my heart want to sing
I will lift my eyes in the darkest night
For I know my Savior lives
And I will walk with you knowing
You'll see me through and sing the songs You give
I can sing in the troubled times
Sing when I win
I can sing when I lose my step
And fall down again
I can sing 'cause You pick me up
Sing 'cause You're there
I can sing 'cause You hear me, Lord
When I call to You in prayer
I can sing with my last breath
Sing for I know
That I'll sing with the angels
And the saints around the throne

—Ed Cash, Chris Tomlin, and Matt Redman.

> I will sing to the Lord all my life; I will sing praise to
> my God as long as I live.
>
> Psalms 104:33

Time marches on and the beat is ever-changing. The future is yet to be written for us all. The past has been one tremendous journey. As I conclude this memoir, my deepest desire is that you have seen God's mercy and grace in my life and, because of that, you are either encouraged in your walk with Christ or you will begin your own journey with Christ if you don't know him as your Lord and Savior. I can say with all assurance that there is a God and that he loves us all; his Son bled and died for us.

I can also say with confidence that my dad gave his heart to Christ. I asked him about this when he was in the hospital a few months prior to his death. He had apologized to my mom for all the hurtful things he had done and told her that he still loved her. I believe this brought healing to them both, and I am grateful. Although I don't excuse his actions toward me, I have forgiven him, and I no longer blame him or God for the abuse.

Maybe you can't understand that kind of forgiveness, but here's the way I now look at things. God gives men free will, and having free will allows us to hurt others. (I myself have abused that authority given me.) Sometimes that hurt is cruel or just pure evil, despicable. But just as God allows free will, he also allows grace, mercy, and healing if we accept it. I can look back and see the good in Daddy's life and know that he accepted that grace. At one point, he may have

TERRY L. SELLERS

been an abuser, but he was also a good provider. He wanted better for his family, and I saw that later in life through his actions and words to me.

He did many things to help others, such as provide free car care for single or widowed women in the church, even though he didn't attend church. He loved to laugh, and he wasn't too proud to admit his wrong in the end. In the weeks just prior to his death, there were several Sundays when just he and I would sit at his kitchen table and talk. He shared many things with me, mostly about his mistakes and regrets. I saw a repentant heart filled with tenderness and love for his family. I'm so thankful for those days that God gave us both.

As for my mom, she was the most giving person I've ever known. She gave when it hurt, although she had so little. If you took it from her by dishonest means, which happened often, she forgave you. She wasn't a materialistic woman, but she found pleasure in the simple things like having her family share a meal together. She never failed to speak of her faith or show concern for one's soul. I never heard her speak badly of others, even ones who constantly mistreated her. In fact, I never heard either of my parents speak badly about each other, even through and after their divorce. They remained friends, and I think that made each of us, their children, better because of it.

I remember the days just prior to her death also, and I see the precious gift from God that it was. It was Christmas, her favorite time of year, and God allowed our family time together that we really hadn't enjoyed in a long while, cherished memories now. There were

things she did for me specifically that holiday, little things like cooking my favorite meal and making my favorite dessert, even though she had so little strength left. It may not seem like much, but I know it was her way of saying thank you and I love you. I only regret that I never told her what it meant to me.

As for me, my song is back, and I sing with more conviction now than ever. "How Can I Keep From Singing (His Praise)"? Just read the words to the song, especially the last stanza. To paraphrase, I sing whether there's victory or defeat, when I fall and when God picks me up. I sing no matter what, and one day I'll sing with the angels, Mama, Daddy, Gram, Pop, Lisa ... all who have gone before me around the throne of my God! But for now, I look forward to my next soul's song.

If I gave the impression in the preceding pages that I had *arrived*, that I've done no wrong or that I'm just a victim, please forgive me. I recently heard a dear friend say that going through a battle doesn't mean you have arrived. It means you should be stronger to go through the next battle. Although I haven't shared, the list of indiscretions in my life is long but they're also covered by the blood. Life is a journey, and on the day I do *arrive*, you won't find me here on earth anymore. I will be singing around the throne!

When I think about situations with my co-workers or even things in the church, my thought is that I've somehow failed them. Often, I allowed my feelings to dictate my actions, but I'm still learning. If I hadn't been so blinded by the attacks against me but instead looked at what the other person might be

TERRY L. SELLERS

going through, I might have been able to offer them the same hope I now have.

As for the walls that I built around me, over time, God has allowed me freedom. God is continually filling my life with wonderful people, and the loneliness that once surrounded me like a life-sucking disease no longer does. In fact, those old friends—loneliness, rejection and alcohol—have been replaced. I am now a friend of God; I am favored by God and I drink the new wine. *Through it all*, God has been faithful. His Word is true!

There is no depth God won't reach to pull me (or you) up to him. There is no distance too far from his mercy, no sin too great for his forgiveness. We're none *worthy of his blood*; it's his gift to us. He will be a *lighthouse* shining out in our darkest night, leading us to safety, and his *grace is truly amazing*. There is *no mountain we can't climb* with him. My God is great; he is my *Rock,* and he'll be yours if he's not already. His love is *unfailing*! He is *my everything*!

When I look back at the first half of my life and what I called my soul's songs, I can now conclude some real truths. While I'm certainly not a teapot, I am clay in the Potter's hands. (*See* Jeremiah 18) He is molding me into a vessel of honor, to be used by and for him. Neither was I nor am I now a lonesome loser, only someone who believed all that the liar said to me. In fact, I was never ever truly alone or without love. The Bible tells me that God is with me to the ends of the earth and that he loved me so much that he sent his only Son to die on a cross for me (and you). That's what I believe now.

The Lord *has* helped me down every road I've ever traveled, even when I was selfish and defiant in my living. Any road I traveled alone, without God, was my own choice to do so. While I did gain a new attitude at a certain point in my life and it was for the positive, it was just superficial. Only God can change the things that matter most. That's what he did in my life and in the lives of my parents. Now my song is truly joyous.

My siblings and I are moving on the best we know how. The one whose marriage was struggling with separation is now back together. The one in trouble with the law is now free of all charges and leading a more law-abiding lifestyle. Unfortunately, the other two are still held captive by their addictions and their poor life choices. When I look at each of them, I see all the good inside. Others often look at their mistakes (most people do), but I know they're good people and they have so much to offer. I long for the day when their lives are placed in the hands of God. Until and *even* then, I will continue to pray.

Although I have said that the past six years have been tough, I would be amiss if I ended this book without saying there have also been so many blessings. One of the greatest blessings is the many gifts of friendship I've acquired along the journey. I've learned that it isn't the things or the possessions that matter most in life but the people you share the journey with, and God has truly put some wonderful people in my life. I'm also blessed to have a good job, a nice home, a dependable car, a loving church family... the list is long. Mostly, I'm blessed to have the best family around, including my parent's siblings and their families.

TERRY L. SELLERS

I don't know your life's story, your soul's songs, but I'm confident that God can rewrite it, most certainly change the tune. It doesn't matter what load of sin or guilt you carry; God is waiting to take it all away. Maybe your pride tells you that this is all just fool's gold, something weak people need and cling to. I say with all confidence, if you believe that, you are deceived by the liar himself. As for me, just call me weak because I believe! The Bible says in 1 Corinthians 1:27 that God uses the weak to confound the strong. Some of you may think me a religious nut, and I'm okay with that too. I *know* my Redeemer lives, and I can't keep it to myself.

You can reject what I say, but in the end, it won't change the truth. I've seen God's hand in my life too much now not to believe that he is real. You can put all of your time and energy into building your kingdom and riches here on earth, but it won't mean a thing in the end. I pray that your pride will step aside before it's too late. I'd rather be wrong in the end and there be no heaven to gain than to be right and for anyone reading this to end up in hell for eternity.

I believe there is a God and that there is only one true God. My God's name is not Allah, or Buddha, or Muhammad. He is not a selfish God or a self-serving God. He is not in a tree; he created the trees. He is not in humanism; he loves all of humanity. He does not hate sinners; he hates sin but loves us all. He is our Trinity. As Jesus, he is our Lord and Savior, our Near Kinsman, our Redeemer, our Rock. There is no other name under heaven by which we can be saved. (*See* Acts 4:12) As our Holy Spirit, he is our Comforter and

our Guide. As our God, he is our Abba Father and our Jehovah Jirah, our God who provides. He is our soon coming King.

None of us will ever deserve the love of God. I sure didn't. We can't earn it. It is a gift, freely given but with a high price and with such love—just like Alex and her necklace. All that is needed to accept this gift is to simply believe that Jesus died for your sins, ask him for forgiveness, and to come live in your heart. It's that simple, and it's for whosoever will.

This has been my personal journey to God and with God. It is an account of his love, mercy, grace, provision, and guidance in my life. It's a sobering thought when I stop and realize that I could have been in hell for over nineteen years now. God has put a song in my heart; I have reason to sing! As I said in the beginning, I'm not a singer, songwriter, or musician, but in heaven, I plan to be all three. Why not? In fact, you're all invited to my concert there. It will be for my God, but you can join me. There's no cover charge. Christ already paid that for you, so won't you come and sing with me for all of eternity to our God?

TERRY L. SELLERS

All I have seen has taught me to trust the creator for all I have not seen.

—Ralph Waldo Emerson

AUTHOR INFO

For further information on Terry Sellers visit her website -

terrysellers.tatepublishing.net

TERRY L. SELLERS